CRITICAL ISSUES IN
ORGANIZATIONS

T0384298

CRITICAL ISSUES IN ORGANIZATIONS

Edited by
STEWART CLEGG AND DAVID DUNKERLEY

Volume 8

LONDON AND NEW YORK

First published 1977 by Routledge

Published 2016 by Routledge

This edition first published in 2013
by Routledge
2 Park Square, Milton Park, Abingdon, Oxon OX14 4RN

Simultaneously published in the USA and Canada
by Routledge
711 Third Avenue, New York, NY 10017, USA

Routledge is an imprint of the Taylor & Francis Group, an informa business

First issued in paperback 2015

British Library Cataloguing in Publication Data
A catalogue record for this book is available from the British Library

ISBN 978-0-415-65793-8 (Set)
eISBN 978-0-203-38369-8 (Set)
ISBN 978-0-415-82293-0 (hbk) (Volume 8)
ISBN 978-1-138-99050-0 (pbk) (Volume 8)
ISBN 978-0-203-54783-0 (ebk) (Volume 8)

CRITICAL ISSUES IN ORGANIZATIONS

Edited by

STEWART CLEGG

and

DAVID DUNKERLEY

ROUTLEDGE DIRECT EDITIONS

ROUTLEDGE & KEGAN PAUL
London, Henley and Boston

First published in 1977
by Routledge & Kegan Paul Ltd
39 Store Street,
London WC1E 7DD,
Broadway House,
Newtown Road,
Henley-on-Thames,
Oxon RG9 1EN and
9 Park Street,
Boston, Mass. 02108, USA
Reprinted in 1978
Printed and bound in Great Britain
by Unwin Brothers Limited,
The Gresham Press, Old Woking, Surrey
A member of the Staples Printing Group
© Routledge & Kegan Paul Ltd 1977

ISBN 0 7100 8506 0

CONTENTS

Chapter 1

INTRODUCTION: CRITICAL ISSUES IN ORGANIZATIONS

Stewart Clegg and David Dunkerley

In the social sciences one can find many volumes whose titles pro-
claim them to be in some sense 'critical'. Indeed, such is the
apparent increased frequency with which such terms are used that
one might be forgiven for supposing them to be of devalued currency.
Yet, here is another volume sufficiently audacious as to claim to
address Critical Issues in Organizations. Such a claim cannot be
lodged lightly. It behoves anyone who proposes it to argue in
what way their volume is 'critical' in such a way as to be distinct
from other contributions.

Many other texts on organizations exist. You may well be
familiar with some of them. If so, then you will be aware of the
bewildering state of disarray that exists in these texts, and which
passes as 'organization theory'. Given the antecedents of organization theory such diversity is hardly surprising. The study of
organizations has developed in a number of specific ways, serving
different ends which have ranged from improving organizational
'effectiveness' to providing theoretical direction for those claim-
ing a purely academic interest. Regardless of the objectives, it
is clear that to speak of a body of 'organization theory' is to
refer to a body of knowledge that, for pragmatic reasons, has developed both unevenly and atheoretically.

Of course, we are not alone in recognizing the problems confronting the analysis of organizations. Such problems pre-occupy
professional conventions and papers. But while similar conclusions
may be reached, the prescriptions suggested are quite dissimilar to
those which we imply. By way of displaying contrast consider the
following example. At the 1974 American Sociological Association
Convention, Jerald Hage pleaded strongly for 'a new wave of attempts
to create general organizational theory' (Hage, 1974, p.19). His
solution was cast in terms of formal middle-range sociological
theory emphasizing theoretical and operational definitions and linkages. Such an analysis presumes a certain value to what has 'preceded it, which we, and our contributors, would question. To
reason as Hage does is to remain secure within the convention of
thesis, whilst neglecting the dialectic of antithesis. To credit
as synthetic a conversation which is conducted entirely within one
thesis concerning the nature of social reality, and the appropriate

way of 'regarding' it, is seriously to devalue the dialectical metaphor.   But the Hage plea is in many respects entirely consistent
with some aspects of contemporary American theorizing in sociology.
The suggested approach would, we suspect, draw heavily upon the
work of methodologists such as Blalock for its 'theory', while its
paramount organizational input would be that style of research
whose hegemony is maintained by the pages of the 'Administrative
Science Quarterly'.

Complementary to, and sometimes in opposition to, the developments and suggestions which emanate from the tradition of 'Administrative Science Quarterly', the study of organizations has pro-
gressed in Europe.   A distinctively European tradition is emergent.
Methodological, theoretical and critical issues which once seemed to
be condemned to silence are being re-awakened, renewed and discussed.   Much of this discussion has centred on the on-going critique currently being developed by members of the 'groupe théore-
tique' of the European Group for Organizational Studies (EGOS).
The group has a short history to date, having emerged from the
first meeting of EGOS in 1975 as a viable focus of interest among
researchers.   Nearly all the contributors to this volume are
currently engaged in this on-going critique.   The focus of the
critique has been on the development of an 'institutional' approach
to the study of organizations, a focus which is represented in
all of the papers collected here.   This speaks to our common commitment to re-awaken some critical issues for discussion.

Our 'issues' - sexism, power, capitalist development, organizational transactions and interactions, the historical interpenetration of state and capital - are not yet found in the indexes
of most texts on organizations.   We hope to remedy this state of
affairs through posing this absence as problematic.   Thus, it
would seem to be no accident that the majority of texts on organization theory place greater emphasis upon concepts such as individual motivation, needs and satisfactions, than upon the structural features of power, exploitation and historical change.
The eagerness with which management theorists have adopted many
of the ideas from organization theory lends further support to the
argument.   However, considering the way in which organization
theory has almost ignored Marx, or interpreted Weber in the nar-
rowest possible way as a progenitor of modern theories of organization structure, then this is not surprising.   The interests of
management and the interests of organization theory have all too
often been in harmony.

A critical theory cannot allow its interest to be so defined.
The function of our papers is to enable one to grasp and understand the reality of that 'life' which organizations find themselves imposed in and on.   As such we distinguish our analyses
from those fictions preserved in the ideology of organization
theory, where the freedom of 'exchanges', 'social constructions',
and the 'satisfaction' of 'needs' reigns dominant.   In contrast,
our papers show contemporary sources of 'unfreedom' as occasioned
through organizations.   We attempt thus to begin conversation
with others who have been both mastered and victimized by the
formulations that we oppose here.

So it is not that our 'critical issues' are 'in organizations'.

They are not.   They are not 'in' organizations in terms of the
wide-spread consciousness of their members, any more than they are
yet 'in' the widespread consciousness of the members of organization theory.   Nor can our issues be constrained 'within' the
boundaries of organizations.   Such closure to social issues and
theory is part of the stance we oppose.   Our issues are 'in
organizations' only in so far as *organization* is the metaphor under
which we collect our thoughts and reflections.   Organization
serves merely as the rubric and the locus of our analysis.   Only
in as much as we constitute them as such are our issues *in* organizations.

   In an organization theory where life has been analysed, paralysed
and reduced to a series of quantifiable variables, our issues would
remain unspoken.   This volume is an attempt to speak this silence.
For all of us, in our various voices, this articulates itself
through redressing the scant consideration given to issues which
are historically located, politically potent, economically relevant,
and socially significant.

   We neither propose to 'synthesize' existing theory, nor to
'broaden' it by importing yet another fledgling sociological stance.
Rather, we propose to overcome existing organization theory.   In
that organizations have been left too much to the ideologists of
administration, their continued existence as an ontological realm
of self-sufficient enquiry has survived critical scrutiny for too
long.   We wish to call into question the continued existence of
such a state of affairs.

   Each of our papers displays this desire in the nature of a
critique which intervenes in the idea of an 'organization theory'.
Our topics and our styles may differ, but our underlying theme,
which stresses what we would call a 'critical' and an 'institutional' approach, remains present in each contribution.

   Janet Wolff's paper takes as its critical issue the topic of
women in organizations.   The paper analyses the social and political movement towards equality of employment for women in the
United Kingdom.   The review leads the writer to the conclusion
that organization theory has been too myopic and apparently unaware
of the wider socio-cultural environment in which organizations
exist.   It cannot account for the 'powerless' role of women in
organizations.   Three important points emerge from the analysis.
First, in spite of extensive recent legislation women are relatively
disadvantaged compared with men in employment.   Second, this
relative disadvantage cannot be accounted for by traditional organization theory.   Third, while a more adequate organization theory
may be constructed, it would be insufficient unless it incorporated
a sociological understanding of extra-organizational factors.   In
spite of these shortcomings detected in organization theory, Janet
Wolff does acknowledge that the theory is able to make some contribution to the understanding of this particular issue.   She
recognizes the movement away from a crude functionalism towards
the attempt to consider meaning in particular situations and to
account for informal as well as formal pressures upon the individual
and the group.   Essentially, the paper is a plea for widening the
scope of organization theory in order to account for social,
political, economic and historical influences within society in

their impact in the organization.   This is a fundamental criticism
of organization theory that other contributors also allude to.

Clegg's paper attacks organization theory at what might be considered to be its least ideological point - its treatment of 'power'
in organizations.   However, he argues that it is in the analysis
of 'power' that the ideology of organization theory is most trans-
parent.   Historically, organization theories of power have developed as a 'language game', in which conventional rules and concepts
of enquiry have foreclosed the possibility of grasping the reality
of power in organizations.   Instead, these conventions have led
organization theorists to substitute what can only be regarded as
'science fictions' for any critical analysis.   Although alternative
concepts and modes of theorizing exist within the tradition of
political analysis, what is most noteworthy is their total neglect
within organization theory.   In distinction to the various versions
of functionalism which organization theory offers as its 'understanding' of power, Clegg proposes the reconsideration of a historically grounded social theory which would question the ontological
assumptions of the organization as a separate reality embedded
within an 'environment'.   Instead of proposing an organization
theory of power for all organizations, irrespective of their institutional location, Clegg proposes that analysis should be in terms
of both wider social formations and specific institutional areas
within these.

Karpik's paper continues the discussion of themes which are
raised in the previous paper.   The broad category of 'capitalism'
as a social formation, a theme of the previous paper, can be discussed in its historical specificity.   Karpik locates the emergence of large technological enterprises as the most developed
moment in the present production of material life.   He refers to
this moment as that of 'technological capitalism'.   The paper
defines its main task as the construction of an analysis which iden-
tifies the rule of functioning of technological capitalism in terms
of the 'capacity' concept of power (puissance).

The paper achieves this by analysing the historical dynamics
which give rise to the transformation of material life into this
specific form of capitalism.   These are the development of a
specific form of the scientific institution, that of heteronomous
science, as the basis of an industrial strategy which realizes
profit within the enterprise neither in terms of 'efficiency' variables belonging to the organization or its environment, nor in
simple modes of surplus value accumulation, but in terms of its
position within an institutional rationality.   This institutional
rationality cuts across any of the conventional categories of
either organization theorists or everyday life.   It is an analytical construct which analyses not *the* organization but the institutional rule of functioning of a diversity of organizations.
This may be seen to display a common rationality which is embedded
within technological capitalism as a specific capitalist form
dependent upon scientifically induced discontinuities.

The analysis serves to exemplify the possibilities of an institutional as opposed to organizational mode of analysis.   Conceived organizationally, either in terms of theory or common sense,
enterprises which constitute the category of technological capit-

alism do not belong together. They are not relatable in any way
other than through .their institutional reality and the underlying
structure that this traces.

McCullough and Shannon present an historical analysis of the
protective role of the state in relation to the growth and decline
of organizations functioning. The state, where it has featured
at all in organization theory, has usually been conceptualized as
little other than a residual environmental or contextual variable.
Such benign indifference could only be born of the general malaise
which has infected recent pluralist theorizing in political science.
Of late, reality has been re-asserting itself, as various crises of
legitimacy concerning state activities at home and abroad have
erupted into our consciousness. The events of May 1968, the war
in Indo-China and its repercussions throughout the world, the
various movements for national liberation - these have all shattered
the innocence which had allowed liberal-pluralist conceptions of a
natural order to flourish in the vacuum where the theory of the
state should be. Naturally occurring crises, just as much as
Garfinkel's ethnomethodological experiments, can have a revelatory
effect by disrupting what passes for normal constituted reality.
McCullough and Shannon use the example of recent events in Northern
Ireland to exemplify the relevance of these remarks for the analysis
of organizations.

The central concern of Wassenberg's paper is to show the inadequacy of current organizational sociology when confronted with
dynamic occurrences at the macro-level. In particular, he makes
reference to its inability to comment in any systematic way on the
recent economic depression in industrialized capitalist states. He
attributes this to the one-sided development of organizational
sociology as primarily focused on static comparative study. This
has resulted in an analytical neglect of organizational 'interactions' and 'transactions'. Static taxonomies have been developed
rather than dynamic models of the actual functioning of interorganizational relations. In order to remedy this situation,
Wassenberg poses as his dominant theme the elaboration of a view
which locates organizational behaviour within a stratified and
dynamic perspective. Wassenberg uses 'stratified' to refer to the
multiple hierarchies of interdependence in which organizations
function. He locates these within a dynamic framework which takes
account of the disparate chronology of organizational location.

It is within this framework that Wassenberg locates the dialectics of 'politicization' and 'professionalization' as opposing
strategies which differentially located institutionalized groups
will attempt to impose upon the organization. This process is
constituted by the three principles of 'bounded interdependence,
rationality and legitimacy'. The development of this model helps
to clarify the nature of organizational transactions. Wassenberg
closes the chapter by posing some interesting new directions in
which a more critical social theory of organizations might develop.

In creating a forum for debate this collection of papers suggests
directions in which organization theory could develop. In the
first instance, we are opposed, at the present, to the kind of synthesis that Hage has argued for. The issue of whether a univer-
sally applicable theory of organizations is possible is highly

problematic.   Our opinion is that at the present stage of development such an exercise would be abortive.   The papers in this volume
point to too many inadequacies in the present state of organization
theory for a synthesis to be meaningful.   Our suggestion is that
these inadequacies should be exposed and debated in order that they
may be overcome.

Second, we see the need for an historical analysis of the development of sociological thought on the concept of organization.   We
argued earlier that, in the way in which it is expounded, organization theory has a 'control' function.   Having this function, it
exists as another metaphor for social order and domination.   Its
function is not new.   Indeed, this was the original function of
theories of 'organic' society and of organization as developed in
the writings of Europeans such as Comte, Saint-Simon and Durkheim.
They turned to sociology to provide an ideology to save their moral
order as a defence in the face of the political and intellectual
upheaval which raged in their contemporary society.   In their
writings we have the germinal seed of present-day organization
theory.   Equally, if we turn to the industrial revolution, here we
see the market theories of possessive individualism and of laissez-
faire emerge as a moral justification for nineteenth-century capitalism.   In time, from these early beginnings, many of the important themes in contemporary organization theory can be seen to have
emerged.

This brings us back to the ideologically committed stance of
organization theory.   As demonstrated above, each of the papers
makes this point in its own way.   The impoverishment of organization theory is due, in part, to its unreflexive and ahistorical
development.   Any synthesis would be impossible at the present
time.

It is clear that the analysis of organizations needs to be sig-
nificantly broadened for any meaningful discourse to take place.
Each of the contributors has made the point that the particular
issue under discussion could only be discussed adequately by going
beyond the existing organizational framework.   Each has argued,
implicitly and explicitly, for a sociology that sees the organization as structurally embedded within the wider social context.
The view of organizations as a series of measurable and related
internal variables normally associated with structure is rejected.
In its place we have a plea for an organizational analysis that is
open-ended, and which recognizes the societal nature of organizational functioning, and which is sensitive enough to respond to
on-going debates outside organizational analysis but within a
wider framework of social theory.

The reader of this volume should be aware that the papers that
comprise it were all written and completed by the end of 1975.
Consequently, there may appear to be some degree of dated-ness in
the text. We feel that this in no way detracts from the theoretical arguments presented.

Chapter 2

WOMEN IN ORGANIZATIONS

Janet Wolff

I

This paper will consider the position of women in organizations, in
particular women at work and women in trade unions. In surveying
the literature available on women's position and progress towards
equality in Britain, I shall argue that traditional sociological
approaches to organizations are inadequate in accounting for the
phenomenon of discrimination and for the persistent fact that
women's position in organizations differs from that of men in the
same organizations. Other papers in this volume demonstrate that
only radically revised forms of organization theory can account
for various phenomena of power in organizations, which cannot
really be explained or analysed simply in terms of organizational
goals, rules or structures. In dealing with the problem of sexism
and female inequality, I shall maintain that even a radically new
starting-point for organization theory will not do. More sophisticated contemporary forms of organization theory go some way
towards understanding the place of women in various organizations.
In order to develop an analysis which is more than partial, however, it is necessary to go outside any organization theory in
order to situate the organization and its structural and ideological features in the macro-social context which it inhabits.
In other words, I shall use this short study of women's place in
organizations to show that (a) women are at a disadvantage in
relation to men in most organizations; (b) organization theory
cannot account for the differential treatment and experience of
the sexes unless its traditional assumptions about the existence,
rationale and functioning of organizations are critically reassessed; and (c) even a modified and sophisticated organizational
approach must be supplemented by a sociological grasp of *extra-*
organizational influences on organizational practice. Women's
position in any organization is inseparable from women's position
in society.

II

It is relevant to start by discussing legislation regarding women,
because clearly if discrimination on grounds of sex becomes illegal,
and, further, if changes in the education system are introduced so
that boys and girls are no longer taught to excel in different areas
and to develop different ambitions and expectations, then this
should be a crucial step in the direction of sexual equality. (For
confirmation of the fact, here taken for granted, that males and
females are essentially similar, and learn to differ, see in particular Ann Oakley (1972) and Department of Employment's Manpower
Paper No. 10 (1974b).)   The abolition of discrimination in employment should eventually mean not only equal pay and equal opportunities but equal status and equal numbers.

The record of recent legislation looks fairly impressive.   In
1970 the Labour Government introduced the Equal Pay Act.   This Act
requires that employers give 'equal treatment as regards terms and
conditions of employment to men and to women'.   It lays down that
women workers must receive the same basic rate where they do the
same work as men.   Employers were given five years to implement
the Act fully, and it should have been fully operative by December
1975.   The Conservative Government of 1970-4 proposed to extend
anti-discrimination legislation and produced a consultative document, 'Equal Opportunities for Men and Women' in October 1973.
The Labour Party in opposition also produced a Green Paper, in
November 1972, entitled 'Discrimination Against Women'.   This
recognized the limitations of the Labour Government's Equal Pay Act,
and, reviewing discrimination in education, training, employment,
politics and the home, put forward twenty-four proposals to eliminate such discrimination.   Back in power, the Labour Party then
proposed a White Paper, 'Equality for Women' in September 1974.
The proposals in this White Paper are implemented in the Government's Sex Discrimination Bill, presented to the House of Commons
in March 1975.   This Bill seeks to make sex discrimination unlawful
in employment, training and related matters (where discrimination on
the ground of being married is also dealt with), education and the
provision of housing and goods, services and facilities to the
public.   It also applies to advertising in these areas and to
aiding and pressure to discriminate, and proposes to set up an
Equal Opportunities Commission to enforce the Bill when it becomes
law.   The White Paper and the Bill do not attempt to deal with all
the proposals in the 1972 Green Paper, but are specifically concerned with women at work and in education and with housing and the
provision of goods: 'The status of women in relation to social
security, taxation, nationality, and matrimonial and family law is
governed by separate legislation and will be so dealt with in the
future' (White Paper, 1974, para. 77).   It is worth noting, too,
that the Labour Party's White Paper makes reference to the consultative document published by the Conservative Party in office
in 1973 (ibid., paras. 22,23), and considers the proposals contained in it 'inadequate both in scope and enforcement' (ibid.,
para. 23).   It therefore sets out to introduce more radical
measures.   (For example, it includes changes in the education
system.   Unlike 'Equal Opportunities', it also covers the police

and prison services.   See National Council for Civil Liberties,
1974b, p.3.)
     Legislation, therefore, appears to have gone a long way towards
enforcing equal conditions of employment for men and women.   But
studies undertaken of particular organizations - factories, commercial and professional organizations and trade unions - leave one
more pessimistic about the power of legislation to achieve such
equality.   This is only partly because of certain inadequacies in
the existing and proposed laws, and I want here to look at some of
these studies and to discuss the achievements of women at work, as
well as the mechanisms which appear to militate against equality.
The point is, of course, that the law can only set down formal
requirements;   the forms taken by discrimination need not be either
illegal or even explicit.   The 1970 Equal Pay Act has turned out
to be notoriously easy to circumvent (see National Council for Civil
Liberties, 1975).   It provides for equal treatment (including pay)
for men and women doing 'the same or broadly similar' work.   The
similarity of the work is judged by a job evaluation study (Equal
Pay Act, 1970 para. 1 (4) and (5)).   Employers can avoid paying the
same wages by differential grading of jobs and maintaining that they
are *not* the same or broadly similar.   The 'Sunday Times' exposed
employers who sent 'secret memos', whose aim was to stop equal pay
for women ('Sunday Times', 4 February 1973, quoted in Comer, 1974,
pp.48-9).   An NCCL report shows how the Act is, or can be, circum-
vented:

     One example is a Shoefayre agreement in 1972, which called male
     shop assistants 'trainee managers' and paid them £3.00 a week
     more than female shop assistants.... In some of these cases ...
     the jobs remain basically the same and only the job titles have
     been changed (National Council for Civil Liberties, 1975, p.8).
The Sex Discrimination Bill, before Parliament at the time of
writing, does not resolve the problem of job evaluation and its
abuses, but attempts to 'reinforce the Equal Pay Act by covering
non-contractual terms and conditions of employment, e.g. training
and promotion' (Labour Party document, 1975).   Again, there are
many let-out clauses for employers.   The Bill excludes single-sex
schools, ministers of religion, employment in a firm of five or less
employees, situations where 'decency' would be preserved if a man
were employed (Sex Discrimination Bill, 1975, para. 7 (2) (b)),
e.g. where sleeping accommodation is not provided for both sexes,
or where men might be in a state of undress.   The general exception
clause (ibid., para. 7 (1)) is worded vaguely enough to allow a lot
of latitude for discrimination.   The law against discrimination
'does not apply to any employment where being a man is a genuine
occupational qualification for the job' or 'to opportunities for
promotion or transfer to, or training for, such employment'.
Women in organizations, then, will not be guaranteed equality in
the near future by legislation and the desire of employers to keep
within the law, or by the operations of the proposed Equal Opportunities Commission (Sex Discrimination Bill, 1975, paras. 45-53).

III

I want now to look at a number of recent studies of women in various
organizations, to consider some of the factors impeding their progress and to discuss the claim that is sometimes made that the
employment of women is expanding in all areas of work and professions, moving towards a greater equality with men, and that there
is a concomitant change in the domestic situation towards what Young
and Willmott (1973) have called 'the symmetrical family'.   To begin
with, a few general statistics about women workers in Britain.   In
June 1971 there were 8,584,000 female employees.   This is 37.8 per
cent of all employees.   Of these female employees, 5,334,000 were
married - 62.1 per cent of the total.   Since 1961, the percentage
of women employees over all employees rose by 2.2 per cent, and the
percentage of married women over all women employees rose by 9 per
cent.   One in three female employees worked 30 hours or less - a
total of 2,757,000.   Between 1961 and 1971, the total number of
female trade union members increased from 1,955,000 to 2,639,000.
As a percentage of all female employees, this represents an increase
from 25 per cent to 33½ per cent in those ten years (Department of
Employment, 1974a).   As well as 8,584,000 female employees, there
were also about 370,000 women who worked as employers or as self-
employed (Central Office of Information, 1975, p.12).   The most
striking statistical fact is the increase in married women return-
ing to employment after motherhood.   The second noteworthy fact
is that the vast majority of women workers is concentrated into a
few industries.   More than half of them work in the three major
service industries: the distributive trades, professional and
scientific services (including teaching and nursing) and miscel-
laneous services (e.g. catering, laundries).   Men are more evenly
spread over the twenty-seven main industrial orders.   In the professions, women predominate in lower-paid jobs.   In 1974, 252 out
of 3,368 barristers in England and Wales were women, 7,000 out of
29,500 members of the National Union of Journalists and 9,000 out
of 26,000 staff of the BBC were women.   In local government, 2
out of 453 chief executives and 32 out of 21,600 chief officers were
women.   Women in business are generally clerks, secretaries, tele-
phone operators, but rarely managing directors or members of the
board of directors (Central Office of Information, 1975, pp.12-23).
   Most of the studies of women at work have been concerned with
middleclass women in business, the professions, the Civil Service
and similar occupations.   Political and Economic Planning, on the
initiative of the Leverhulme Trust, commissioned a number of such
studies in 1966 (see Fogarty,Rapoport and Rapoport, 1971, p.30).
An exception is Jephcott's 'Married Women Working' (Jephcott, Seear
and Smith, 1962) which looks at the employment of women at Peak
Frean's biscuit factory in Bermondsey.   The research is sometimes
carried out within an organization, investigating the jobs women
hold there and also the home background of those women (e.g.
Fogarty, Allen, Allen and Walters, 1971);   some studies, on the
other hand, take a particular sample of women workers in Britain,
and proceed to raise questions about their place of work, conditions of employment, domestic arrangements, etc (e.g. Klein,
1965).   The complementarity provides an overall picture, illus-

trated by detailed analysis in selected areas, of the meaning behind
the statistics quoted above.   The picture is one of a society where
an increasing number of women, particularly married women, goes to
work and returns to work after marriage and child-bearing; employers
increasingly require to call on this labour force, and to adapt to
its particular needs, for example by providing part-time employment;
and women have been making a certain, albeit very limited, entry
into hitherto male areas of employment.   What also emerges, and
this is the concern of this paper, is that many factors still militate against women's equal treatment with men.   This means that
even where there is formal equality, where there are no explicit
barriers to women's employment and promotion (and it is, after all,
formal equality that present legislation attempts to guarantee),
there are still enough constraints and restrictions to ensure that
women do not have an equal chance with men to reach the top or to
be successful.   The most important impediments are: (i) the
attitudes of management and employers; (ii) the nature of the work,
including hours, arrangements for leave and lack of possibilities
for later training for women; (iii) attitudes and expectations of
women themselves, and the relationship of their attitudes to work
and their attitudes to domestic commitment; (iv) more fundamental
differences which do exist between the sexes, justifying differential treatment in organizations, and which begin with the earliest
socialization of girls and their experiences in education.   None
of these problems is solely a question of intra-organization practice, though the first two are to some extent comprehended in the
framework of organization theory.   The last two can only be grasped
in an extra-organizational perspective.

A Department of Employment survey has recently been carried out
by Audrey Hunt (Hunt, 1975), investigating employment policy of
managers in Britain regarding women.   The survey covered many
different types of establishment and organization, and discovered
widespread prejudices against women.   A quarter of the formulators
of personnel policy, and a third of implementers, are in favour of
equal pay, more women in senior positions and more access to training.   Most managers responsible for hiring begin with the belief
that a women is likely to be inferior to a man as an applicant, in
appearance, ability or qualifications.   Hunt found that managers
were likely to oppose the establishment of equal opportunity, and
that they thought the male working pattern was the norm, so that,
since these hours or career patterns did not suit women, women
would have to suffer.   This survey appears almost twenty years
after Myrdal and Klein wrote:

The economic need is likely in the long run to be more effective
than all the social arguments ... in convincing employers and
public authorities that something has to be done, in terms of
working hours, training courses and the creation of social
amenities, to enable married women to accept employment (Myrdal
and Klein, 1956, p.163).

It has been generally argued, in most of the surveys of women's
employment, that economic expansion gave the greatest possible
boost for jobs for women and put pressure on employers to adapt
their working conditions to women's available hours and years.
Myrdal and Klein, Jephcott et al., Klein and the Political and

Economic Planning studies recommend that employers adapt to women's
needs.

> There thus is a strong case for reviewing employment policies for
> both industry and other types of work so as to extend the oppor-
> tunities for part-time jobs (Jephcott Seear and Smith, 1962,
> p.174).
> From the community's point of view women are of great importance
> both as workers and as wives and mothers, and it would seem
> necessary to provide them with the facilities to perform both of
> these functions simultaneously and effectively so that neither
> their homes nor their jobs suffer unduly from this duality or
> role.... It would seem that, if firms are to meet their labour
> demands in the future, more and more will have to raise their
> egalitarian policies and be prepared to make concessions (Klein,
> 1965, p.134).

This, it is argued, is as much in the interests of the economy and
the employers as of the women themselves.

> It is clear that there are good economic grounds ... for enlarg-
> ing the field so as to give women too their chance of selection
> for the top.... In so far as women's work abilities and interests
> cover the same range as men's, it is in employers' and the econ-
> omy's interest that women with great ability should have the
> chance to replace men of less ability (Fogarty, Rapoport and
> Rapoport, 1971, p.483).

This is not only in order to make the most efficient use of talent
at the top of the professional and occupational scale, as the last
statement maintains.   (The main concern of the PEP studies was how
best use could be made of the country's reserve of highly qualified
women, ibid., p.510.)   It is also, more generally, because acknow-
ledging this additional source of female labour (particularly older,
married women, who have traditionally been either absent from, or
disadvantaged in, the labour market) will make for more economic
and efficient running of the organization and will aid economic
expansion.   Thus, generally held views that women and part-timers
are more unreliable, have higher turnover and absentee rates, and
are less able to do the job than men (or, in some cases, single
and/or full-time women) are challenged.   (See, for example,
Department of Employment, 1975, Ch. 5; Klein, 1965, pp.112-20.)
The Department of Employment survey concludes:

> Generally there is scope for part-timers to be offered jobs in
> a wider range of occupations and at higher levels of skill and
> responsibility especially if an effort is made - for example
> by the use of flexi-time - to adapt the conditions of the job
> to the needs of the workers concerned.   Employers may find
> benefits in reduced absence and turnover and better performance
> generally;   and they may be able to find levels of talent and
> skill on a part-time basis not available to them in the full-
> time labour market.... The trend towards part-time employment
> for married women seems a strong and irreversible one and the
> employer who turns his (sic) back on it is opting out of a
> large and expanding field of labour supply (pp.56-7).

Why have employers, even by 1975 (the time of Audrey Hunt's study)
failed to recognize what is in their own interests, and what is
inevitable and 'irreversible'?   One obvious point to make, of

course, is that the assumption of full employment and economic
expansion can no longer be made, as it was by Fogarty et al. and
by Klein a few years earlier.   In the present period of recession
and unemployment, women, and particularly part-time workers (a
third of female workers in 1972), are usually among the first to
be laid off.   With the formal requirement for equal pay, neither
is there any point in hiring women instead of men where they can
do the same job for less money.   But of course there is more to
the question than the current economic situation.   The fact that
there was need for legislation, and the discoveries of the Political
and Economic Planning and other surveys, suggest more fundamental
forms of discrimination which can be expected to operate even in
periods of expansion.   I take Fogarty's study of women in top jobs
(Fogarty, Allen, Allen and Walters, 1971) here, to consider more
closely the way women succeed and fail in higher levels of employment.

The book comprises four studies: women in two companies, women
directors, women in the BBC and women in the administrative class
of the Civil Service.   In all cases, the proportion of women at
the top was small.   The researchers set out to discover why, in
some cases interviewing the women themselves (the study of women
directors) and in some cases interviewing men too (men who worked
in the two companies, male administrators in the Civil Service).
The case of the Civil Service is particularly interesting.   The
Civil Service has been in the forefront among employers in the
drive towards sex equality in employment.   A bar against married
women was dropped in 1946.   In 1955, agreement was reached on
the implementation of equal pay in the Civil Service in seven annual
instalments.   Fogarty et al. (1971) point out that since that date
the Civil Service has treated sex differentiation in its employment
practices and the working life of the Service as a non-issue
(p.238).   Nevertheless, they say:

> When one looks at the administrative, executive and clerical
> classes separately it becomes clear that the pattern of female
> employment in the Service reflects that within society at large,
> women have moved in greatest numbers into the low status jobs
> whilst males have moved into higher status employment (p.239).

In the other three studies this is more to be expected, for the
researchers found explicit prejudices against women (even, in the
BBC, prejudice against married women on the part of single women).
They found that the nature of work made it difficult, if not impossible, for women to succeed.   For example, the problems encountered by women directors in Board meetings and the 'mysterious male
rites' of the City (p.98) prevent them from carrying out their work
on the same footing as men.   The same problem of a 'male world'
exists at the BBC, particularly in areas like current affairs and
in outside broadcasts, where working with a largely or exclusively
male technical team in a position of authority has its own special
problems: 'The Editor said to me: no film crew wants to be told
what to do by a woman' (p.196). The 'maleness' of work is more
pervasive than this, too:

> It was felt generally that the socializing, the drinking in the
> right pubs and clubs, and above all the easy social contact which
> men have with one another, all militated against the advancement

of women.   All these contacts were felt to give men much more
opportunity of indulging in internal politics than women could
ever have (p.197).

In the Civil Service, however, there is no equivalent division into
male and female worlds.   The commitment to impartiality ensures
that men and women are judged solely in terms of their demonstrated
merit, and also that members of either sex cannot use traditional
techniques to get ahead unfairly, such as 'sitting on the boss's
knee' or 'drinking with the boys' (p.256).   Nevertheless, even the
Civil Service appears to have to capitulate to the sexism of the
outside world:

> The closest link appears to operate within the Ministry of Defence
> where arguments about the impropriety of women operating in a
> man's world appear both to have made women administrators in the
> Ministry a rare occurrence and to have encouraged male members of
> the Ministry to a somewhat patronizing attitude towards women
> administrators encountered in the course of their work.   Some
> other ministries face the dilemma of whether, initially at least,
> they should affront the susceptibility of their clients by
> presenting them with a women administrator (p.274).

Even in a situation where formal equality of the sexes is explicitly
stated, then, the result is still an unequal situation.   This has
a lesson to teach, of course, about the potential efficacy of the
Equal Pay Act and prospective legislation for equal opportunities.
As Fogarty et al. conclude with regard to the administrative class
of the Civil Service:

> It does seem that within the rules of the formal organization of
> the administrative class which enshrine equality of opportunity
> for the sexes, the understandings, attitudes and mores which are
> part of the texture of the informal organization of the class
> operate to steer women away from the scenes of important action
> and hence lessen the likelihood of their being seen as candidates
> for top posts (p.303).

The contemporary situation of women in organizations is clear. Women
have been employed during the last decade or so in larger numbers
than ever before.   In some cases, the barriers to formal equality
with men have been removed or modified.   Nevertheless, they have
not achieved equality at work, and neither does new and proposed
legislation guarantee any swift move towards such equality.   The
proportion of women at the top of their respective careers is minute
in relation to the proportion of workers who are women.   Organizational and ideological constraints operate to make promotion and
success far more difficult for women than for men.   On the lower
levels of the employment market, there is also enormously differential treatment of the sexes.   Women workers are concentrated
into certain types of industry and employment and are greatly under-
represented in most of the rest.   Employers' attitudes have been
shown to be as important in the factory as in the top levels of
administration.   Jephcott (Jephcott, Seears and Smith, 1962,
pp.68-77) cites the prejudice of managers against women workers and
against part-time workers, on the grounds of assumed unreliability
and inefficiency - arguments which she demonstrates are without
foundation.   Because of the persistence of a widespread unwilling-
ness to adapt the work situation to the needs of potential workers

(flexi-time, part-time, maternity leave, etc.), the plea of Myrdal
and Klein in 1956 has gone largely unheeded. They said:

> It is our conviction that the only constructive approach to the
> problem of women in employment is to treat the organization of
> work, rather than of the women workers, as variable.... We have
> to ask, 'What are the working conditions most conducive to max-
> imum efficiency, considering the fact that workers have home
> responsibilities as well as jobs and that married women, in par-
> ticular, often have arduous as well as important responsibilities
> at home?' (Myrdal and Klein, 1956, p.93).

It is not simply a question of employers' attitudes and prejudices
in appointing and promoting. Just as important, and just as detri-
mental to women's advancement, is the fact that the organization
of work and the demands of the job effectively rule out women as
applicants in the first place. Coupled with this is the lack of
training and apprenticeships for women. (The percentage of girls
aged 15-17 entering apprenticeships to skilled occupations in 1972
was 15.2 per cent of the total. Nearly 80 per cent of this 15.2
per cent were apprentice hairdressers and manicurists (see Department of Employment, 1975, p.5).) Women workers confront a situation where they often start with the disadvantage of few prospects
of training for a job, the problem of being unable to fulfil the
requirements to perform the job with the same full-time commitment
as men (because of domestic commitments) and a more fundamental
block in the form of male prejudice against female labour in 'male'
jobs. I want to argue, however, that there is far more to the
problem of discrimination. These factors are all, in a sense,
built into the organization of work, employment and interaction in
the establishment; they are, indeed, the primary concern of the
studies I have reviewed. The analysis is limited, for it does not
take account of the two other factors I referred to earlier: namely
the attitudes and expectations of women workers themselves, and the
differential socialization and education of boys and girls *into*
male and female roles and jobs. Neither does it take the fact of
'women's two roles' as problematic. The suggestion that employers
should be more flexible in the employment of married women because
of the latter's 'arduous responsibilities' in the home is based on
the assumption that women's other (domestic) role is sacred and
inviolable. In the next section, I shall try to deal with the
extra-organizational constraints on women as workers, and discuss
this question of 'two roles' in the context of the social definition of women.

It should be noted that women's inferior position in organizations is not confined to work. Women workers are under-represented
in trade unions, and there are disproportionately few among union
officials, lay and full-time. Some 2 out of the 38 members of the
General Council of the TUC are women, occupying reserved places
(Report of the 44th Women Workers Conference 1974, which in 1975
recommended that this be increased to 3). The chairman of the TUC
in 1974-5 was a woman, 1 of only 5 women chairmen in more than 100
years. There are presently (TUC, 1975) 2.6 million women members
within the TUC, representing 26 per cent of the total membership.
At the 1974 TUC Congress, 84 out of 1,030 delegates were women
(only 8.4 per cent). A survey on the position of women in unions

affiliated to the TUC showed that, in the 62 organizations that
replied (representing nearly 2.5 million women), 1 member in 3 is
a woman, but only 1 full-time official in 32 is a woman.   There
are 71 women and 2,259 male full-time officials (TUC, 1975, p.39).
There is, to date, no systematic study of the position of women in
trade unions and the processes of advancement, election and appoint-
ment as they affect female trade unionists. While this remains to
be investigated, it is reasonable to suppose that similar discrim-
inatory factors are at work as those in women's employment: a combination of inconvenience of hours and commitment for married women,
male prejudice about women's capabilities, and limited confidence
and aspirations on the part of women themselves.

IV

So far, I have considered constraints within organizations which
affect women's advancement towards equality with men.   The central
thesis of this paper is that these must be viewed in the light of
more general social constraints on women, and in the context of
women's position in society.   The Labour Party recognized the
limitations of legislation regarding equality at work:
> A woman will obtain little benefit from equal employment oppor-
> tunity if she is denied adequate education and training because
> economic necessity or social pressures have induced her to enter
> the labour market at an early age.   Some mothers will derive
> as little benefit if there is inadequate provision for part-time
> work or flexible working hours, or for day nurseries (White
> Paper, 1974, para. 21, p.5).
It proposed to deal separately with the question of social security
and pensions (para. 25).   It stated (para. 26) that the law should
not attempt to deal with personal and intimate relationships. In
other words, the government did not intend to interfere in the area
of roles within the family.   It was certainly correct in recognizing the limitations of the proposed legislation, for sex-roles
in the family determine and direct sex-roles outside it.

Myrdal and Klein (1956) discussed the problems faced by married
women and working mothers.   Taking as given the fact that, for the
most part, women do have 'two roles', they support the right and
need of women to work, and demonstrate their ability and reliability
as employees.   Their contention is that employers must acknowledge
the particular needs of married women employees and adapt the work
situation to them as far as possible.   (In the meantime, however,
they recommend (p.157) that girls be advised to be realistic, and
train for 'women's jobs', like teaching, shopkeeping, dressmaking,
which are more easily combined with marriage and motherhood!)   Now,
I would question this kind of solution.   To some extent, it is true
that shortening working hours, allowing paid maternity leave, etc.,
will accelerate a move towards equality.   But as long as sociologists still talk of *women's* two roles, it is clear that women will
remain at a disadvantage in their organizations, whether occupational or trade unions.   Where it is the woman's responsibility to
run the home, look after the children, take time off work when they
are ill or on holiday from school, it is inevitable that the man

will continue to be the main breadwinner, and that the woman's job
will be secondary (both to her primary role and to her husband's
job).   Whatever radical changes employers institute, they will be
unable to employ women on the same basis as men.   Women with young
children will be unable to spare the time for union activity, for
travel on behalf of their organization, for occasions which neces-
sitate working at night.   They will have to continue to be 'realistic'.

Young and Willmott (1973) have recently argued that the family
is on the way to becoming 'symmetrical';   that women are becoming
more committed to their outside work, and men are doing more work
in the house.   This is not the place to criticize their methodology, or the assumptions upon which this statement rests, but they
have certainly not managed to prove their hypothesis (see Bell,
Firth and Harris, 1974).   The Principle of Stratified Diffusion
which they adopt (basically, the belief that what the elite does
today, the lower orders will do tomorrow) is dubious, to say the
least;   further, it is far from clear that the elite *is* practising
sexual equality in the family.   It is still, after all, 'maternity'
not 'paternity' leave which is generally requested of employers,
though all the evidence shows that fathers (or, for that matter,
friends or other relatives) are as capable of looking after children
as the biological mothers, without emotional harm to the children
(see Rutter, 1972).   Advertising of food and domestic goods and
appliances is still directed primarily at women.   Rising prices
are still said to affect 'the housewife'.   Pressure for nurseries
attached to places of work is predominantly from or on behalf of
women, who might thereby take their infants and small children with
them when they go to work.   In short, women still have 'two roles',
and men do not.   (Men are, of course, husbands and fathers, as
much as women are wives and mothers.   Their domestic role, however,
is not an occupational one in competition with extra-domestic occupations, in the same way as that of their wives.)   And women's
role in organizations is interconnected with their role at home.
If the family *were* 'symmetrical', one could begin to talk about the
possibility of real equality at work.   The years of caring for
small children, the problem of time to do the shopping, to collect
older children from school, to care for sick children and older
relatives, would be the shared and equal responsibility of men and
women.   As things are, we can only agree with Ann Oakley (1974,
pp.79-80) when she says: 'Marriage, and housewifery, are basic
impediments to occupational sex-equality.   The female professional
worker is likely to differ in one important respect from the male
professional worker: she is between three and four times more
likely to be unmarried.'   The plea for more part-time and re-
training schemes is not enough in itself to eradicate differences
in the treatment of male and female employees.   Women are not in
a position to take advantage of 'equal opportunities' at work.
Attention to purely internal organizational factors, like the prejudice of managers, training schemes, hours of work and the like,
will neither explain nor resolve the problem of inequality.   And it
follows that a sociological approach which focuses on the organization itself, like the studies we have considered, can only ignore
or take as unalterable 'women's dual role'.   It cannot begin to
account for unequal treatment and disparities of achievement.

V

There is another yet more fundamental reason why women in organizations can only be studied within a macro-social perspective.   It
is not simply that women have a practical conflict of duties which
prevents them from having the same commitment to work (or union
politics) as that of men, for behind this lies the pervasive ideology of sex-roles and sexual identity.   A society which places
central value on the monogamous, heterosexual, nuclear family
ensures thereby that men and women do define their expectations and
ambitions in the context of the family.   One aspect of the ideology
of sex is the notion of 'femininity'.   Certain ways of behaving
(aggressive, ambitious, over-confident, intellectual) are not felt
to be feminine qualities.   Certain types of work are accepted as
women's work (catering, dressmaking, nursing, social work, teaching,
rather than engineering, for example).   Women's work is, in effect,
an extension of the kind of work women do in their primary role -
at home.   It is concerned with servicing, as secretaries or cooks,
with care of children and the sick, with food, clothing and socialization.   It has been established that there is little or no biological basis for differentiation of work by sex (see Oakley, 1972;
Department of Employment, 1975).   Similarly, any acquaintance with
cross-cultural studies by anthropologists confirms that the notion
of 'femininity' is culturally relative (Oakley, 1972;   Mead, 1935,
1962).   As Oakley says:
    Men and women *are* temperamentally different.   But what does
    this 'fact' mean?   It means that personality differences between
    male and female exist within Western society with a certain
    constancy and stability.   But it does not mean that these dif-
    ferences are moulded by biology - indeed, it says nothing at all
    about how much of the difference is due to biology and how much
    to culture (op. cit., p.50).
She looks at societies where the roles, personalities and characteristics of the sexes are reversed - the Tchambuli, studied by
Margaret Mead, where the women are self-assertive, practical and
managing and the men do the shopping, carve, paint and dance and
wear ornaments;   the Bamenda people, where the women do the heavy
agricultural work;   and the Zuni Indians, among whom the women are
aggressive and the male 'faces the wedding night with fear and
trembling' (p.57).   After reviewing a number of studies of small
children in England and the USA, their treatment by their parents
and their learning experiences at school, she concludes that initial
similarity between boys and girls is transformed into a noticeable
difference by the age of puberty.   Boys learn to become assertive,
active, numerate, technically inventive.   Girls begin to 'under-
achieve' academically at adolescence, and start to conform to the
female stereotype.   By then, they have acquired traditional expectations about their future roles, the vast majority (according to
one study of 600 girls) having no ambition or expected achievement
other than marriage and home-making (p.86).   They become more
'feminine' in interests, behaviour and expectations.   Her conclusion about the supposed innateness of such a dichotomy of personalities is as follows:
    If gender has a biological source of any kind, then culture makes

it invisible.   The evidence of how people acquire their gender
identities ... suggests strongly that gender has no biological
origin, that the connections between sex and gender are not
really 'natural' at all (pp.187-8).

Girls are thus taught to be 'female'.   And what it is to be female
is a socio-cultural definition, and one which varies cross-
culturally.   In our society, girls are socialized in conformity
with their primary future role of wife/mother, and this begins at
birth.   This means that no amount of equality of pay, training or
opportunities will actually make women equal with men in the work
situation.   They have already learned too thoroughly to excel in
the wrong qualities, and to be deficient in most of the qualities
which are essential for most higher occupations.   Furthermore, one
of the things they have learned is not to *want* to be doctors, directors, architects, barristers or engineers.   They have not taken
advantage of school or higher education to qualify themselves for
the scientific, commercial or professional jobs which boys had been
taught to expect and to aim for.   Ten years later, an egalitarian
employment policy will not do them much good.   Not only are the
skills and knowledge not developed; women who are qualified for a
particular job characteristically lack the confidence to apply for
it, or to seek promotion (see, Fogarty, Rapoport and Rapoport, 1971;
and Fogarty, Allen, Allen and Walters, 1971).   It is not only
formal rules and structure which must be altered to permit equality.
The whole societal ideology of sex-roles would need to be revolu-
tionized.   Women will only force entry into the male worlds of
work and politics if they are motivated to do so, and so far it has
always been an exceptional minority which has been so motivated.

It would be deviating too much from the subject of women's place
in organizations to continue to pursue the broader question of the
education and motivation of girls and women, but it must be stressed
that under-achievement at work is intimately connected with under-
achievement in education and all extra-domestic activities.   I have
been concerned to show that the role of women in organizations
differs from that of men, and that pressures are at work to keep
women in an inferior and precarious position.   This is not simply
an organizational problem, however.   It is as inseparable from the
fact of women's subsidiary role in society as a whole as managers'
employment prejudices against women are inseparable from their
basic sexist attitudes in everyday life.   If we really want to
understand why women are usually the secretaries, nurses and lower
administrators in many organizations, or why they are under-
represented or totally absent in others, and if we are serious
about effecting equality and equal opportunity, then to ignore this
connection would be either naive or hypocritical.   In this particular case, organizational practices are very much integrated into,
and determined by, social practices and ideological factors.   Ability, availability and personality are the crucial stumbling blocks
for women's advancement in organizations, and each is the result of
sex-typing and gender-learning.   Underlying all this - the social
basis for the whole ideological structure - is the family.   The
primacy of the nuclear unit of man, woman and children dictates the
role of women and, consequently, the processes of socialization
which ensure the persistence of the 'feminine mystique' (Friedan,
1965) essential for the continued existence of the family.

VI

Women's role in organizations can be explained to a limited extent
by looking at the organizations themselves and the formal and
informal processes at work in them.   In an earlier section, I discussed the constraints of a working-day which is unsuitable for
married women workers, the impediment of management prejudices and
opposition, and the more subtle obstacles of closed 'male worlds'
which exclude women from part of the job.   A sociology which analyses the organization in an open-minded and sensitive manner can
detect such factors.   Organization theory has developed its tools
and techniques beyond a crude functionalism, and is able, for
example, to consider the meanings and orientations of actors within
organizations (Silverman, 1970), and to recognize that organizational structures are the result of inter-individual practices.
It is also sophisticated enough to take account of informal as well
as formal processes operating in the organization (Dunkerley, 1972,
p.40).   This is important where, as I have been arguing, formal
equality does not ensure operative equality.   Thus, implicit prejudices may be revealed, and informal rules and practices, which
exclude women, may be detected.   This is as far as one can go
within organization theory.   The constraints operating on women in
organizations originate not merely in the organizations themselves
but in society.   Within the perspective of organization theory, we
can see how long hours and inflexible working time militate against
the employment of women with 'two roles', but we cannot discuss the
basic question of *why* women have two roles.   We can refer to the
'informal' prejudices operating in respect of women's promotion
prospects, but we cannot perceive those ideological influences which
discourage women from taking advantage of whatever opportunities
there are, nor can we understand their origin.   The very question
of women's role and position in organizations can only be answered
by a macro-sociology which situates the organization in the society
which defines its existence, goals and values.

This paper has discussed the contemporary situation of women and
their prospects for equality with men in organizations, in the light
of government legislation and with regard to certain studies of
women at work.   Out of this, we have drawn a number of conclusions.
First, women are disadvantaged vis-a-vis men in organizations.
Second, legislation alone will not be able to effect equality.
Third, wider social change must precede or accompany changes in
organizational practice (e.g. equal pay, flexi-time, etc.).   Last,
organization theory is only partially adequate in comprehending
this problem and its solution.

NOTE

I would like to thank Alan Warde, Bob Towler, Helen Barnes, Lee
Comer and Lewis Minkin for useful discussions while I was writing
this paper, and for helpful comments on it.

Chapter 3

POWER, ORGANIZATION THEORY, MARX AND CRITIQUE

Stewart Clegg

I

Recent interventions in the debate concerning the concept of 'power' (Lukes, 1974; Clegg, 1975) have stressed that the most potent type of power is that which is rarely exercised. I have discussed this as the way in which we may be so embedded within the iconic theorizing power of a particular form of life, a particular form of domination, that an unthinking, unthought consensus reigns supreme in our daily life. The order of a particular interest theorizes the possibility of whatever issues arise for power to be exercised over in such a way that the security of the ruling convention and interest is rarely disturbed. What Gramsci (1971) calls 'hegemony' is thus preserved.

In this chapter I want to continue enquiry into these themes through confronting the theory of organization power with the power of organization theory. I will argue that the texts of organization theory share a mutual interest with the world they purport to depict. Their explanations are merely glosses which simply serve to reproduce this world. They do not account for this world, nor can they. In their theorizing, just as in the theorizing that is that organization that they attend to, these texts exhibit an 'interest'. This interest is not so much written about, as shown in the topic. Thus, I wish to treat what the topic says as somewhat less important than what the topic shows. Elsewhere, I have formulated this in the following terms:

> In attending to the various ways in which theorists have approached and used the concept of power, then, we are attending not only to their definitions and the critiques of these, but to the 'theorizing power' which makes of such definitions and critiques orderly, recognizable and sociological phenomena. The air of authenticity which they wear as plausible scholarship is a manifestation of their mode of production. The actual writing merely re-presents and preserves the deeper possibility of how it is that they are at all possible. Their possibility as features of the sociological enterprise to be discussed, argued, debated and criticized is rooted in their methodical character. They result from the theorists' engagement with method, and are only

possible given the theorists' engagement with a tradition of
theorizing (Clegg, 1975, pp.10-11).

As a manifestation of a mode of production any theoretical product is the objectification of expended labour time spent in the
interest of a specific intellectual capital.   In this chapter I
want to propose that the practice of organization theory re-presents
a particular interest as its intellectual capital, and that this is
the interest of Capital.

One almost banal way of doing this would be to point to what
organization theory says in its products.   But it produces a very
differentiated batch of commodities so that what might be true of
'Taylorism' or 'Fordism' (Gramsci, 1971; Benyon, 1973) may not apply
as a general ascription.   Any such ascription ought not make reference to the individual motivations of particular theoretical pro-
ducers.   To do so would be both impertinent and impossible.   Impertinent, because it would offend the sensibilities of many good
people who are sincere in their craft.   Impossible, because I have
no knowledge of other people's intentions other than that which I
can conventionally assume or construct (Wittgenstein, 1968).

Much of the produce of organization theory has been developed at
the interface of capitalist theory and capitalist practice in the
academic institutions of business.   Here it provides both a market
and a meeting place for theoreticians and organizers.   For these
organizers it functions as a part of the rhetoric of rule, encap-
sulated in O & M, work study, job evaluation and the rest.   As
such, it is assuredly a theory for the organizers of the organized.

But this is still too mechanical, too much of a caricature.   An
assertion which blighted one because of one's paymaster would leave
organization theorists in esteemed historical company (think of
Marx's reliance on Engel's profits!).   It would be as if one were
to be ensnared because of the application by others of a practice
which one may have been engaged in producing, but not utilizing.
But now we are getting nearer the kernel.   It may not be the *application* of the practice as such, but the *potential* of the practice,
a practice which ironically denies potential.

With the notion of the potential of the practice we begin to
return to the idea of its 'theorizing power'.   If the possibility
of the theoretical product is ordained by the theorizing power which
rules its production, then this theorizing power will also circum-
scribe the potential (and non-potential) of the practice the theoretical product enables.   In this sense the theorizing power in
which a tradition is trapped (which traps a tradition) will open and
close specific possibilities through the presences and absences of
its problematic (Althusser, 1969).

Through theorizing the absence of a critical concept of 'power'
within organization theory one can grasp that which both forecloses
the possibility of a radical problematic and preserves the hegemony
of capitalist theorizing as the problematic of its tradition of
discourse (Theorizing For Capital).

For sociology this hegemony must be confronted by criticism.   As
Gramsci (1975) reiterates in his Letters, criticism involves the
confrontation of the political significance of an intellectual practice with the way in which it is formulated. (1)   Gramsci recom-
mends that a decisive critical confrontation with an intellectual

practice will be one that is made against its 'great intellectual'.
This is to commit the error of intellectual fetishism.   Ideas may
be embodied in thinkers, but thinkers are but moments in the tra-
dition(s) of thought.   The attack must be made not on the 'great
intellectual' but on what *enables* his existence, what *enables* his
intellectual productions, and his silences.   And these presences
and absences are those of a specific historical discourse.

A critical confrontation cannot be made by speaking within the
terms of a tradition of discourse.   To speak thus is to let these
terms theorize for us (as Althusser, 1969, p.94, argues).   Neither
can criticism choose to ignore current practice because of its
debilitating tone, any more than it can speak that tone.   It must
intervene and interrupt a stream of discourse, as Torode (1975) has
argued.

One way of interrupting organization theory would be to attempt
to retrieve its essential forgetfulness of its historical location
and genesis.   One feature of this discourse has been that while it
speaks of 'power' it has never grasped 'power' in any radical sense.

Theorizing from *in power*, from *in control*, it has never confronted *Being under power*, *Being under control*.   Being under power
flickers out of focus through the lens that organization theory
would have us use.   It will be seen that its view presumes a specific and historically recent ontology.   Macpherson (1973) argues
that our European tradition presents us with an older ontology
which enables us to connect with being under power, being under
control.

II

The development of a specific concern with 'power' in the theory
of organizations is related to the post-Hawthorne 'discovery' of
the informal organization (Roethlisberger and Dickson, 1939; Landsberger, 1958).   Prior to this the usual focus of enquiry was the
structure of formal authority, as Thompson suggests:

the usual definitions of power are properly applicable to the
internal structures of formal organizations.   One reason why
research workers have seldom regarded actual power in such organizations may be that the classics on bureaucracy have stressed
the rational aspects of organization, with emphasis on authority
to the neglect of unauthorized or illegitimate power.   And it
was not long ago that informal organization was 'discovered' in
bureaucracies (Thompson, 1956, p.290).

Thompson indicts the 'classics of bureaucracy' for their neglect
of 'power' to the benefit of 'authority'.   As Weber's work represents the essential 'classics of bureaucracy' for most sociologists,
one might think that Weber is responsible for the neglect of 'power'
in organization theory - except that Weber is so frequently cited
as the source of a concern with 'power'.   This seeming anomaly is
explicable when one considers the context in which Weber's 'classics
of bureaucracy' were translated and incorporated into American
sociology.

Weber's work on 'power' and 'authority' became available to most
organization theorists through Parsons and Henderson's translation

known as 'The Theory of Social And Economic Organization' (Weber, 1947).   In a much remarked upon footnote by Parsons (Weber, 1947, p.152), the concept of *herrschaft* is translated as 'authority', thus preserving what Gouldner (1970) has called Parsons's 'superordinate' view of power, as if it were Weber's. (2)   This 'superordinate' concept leads Parsons to regard 'power' and 'authority' in two ways:
  either as two different stages in development, in which, for
  instance, power is viewed as the degenerate or the immature form
  of authority; or as two alternative ways in which one person or
  group can structure the behaviour of others.   In both cases they
  are viewed as mutually exclusive, as if, when one exists, the
  other does not.... If it had been looked at from the standpoint
  of *subordination* in the social world, power and authority would
  more likely be viewed as dual structures, both *simultaneously*
  present, in subtle and continual interaction.   Power, in short,
  exists not simply when authority breaks down, or before authority
  has had a chance to mature.   It exists as a factor in the lives
  of subordinates, shaping their behaviour and beliefs, at every
  moment of their relations with those above them.... Legitimacy
  and 'authority' never eliminate power; they merely defocalize
  it, make it latent (Gouldner, 1970, p.294).
     In those studies which have followed Parsons's 'view' of 'power' as a 'superordinate' concept, then 'power' relates to 'authority' as something distinct, as something 'informally' rather than 'formally' developed.   This becomes the theme for the development of organization-theory studies of power.   For instance, Bennis et al. (1958) follow this view in noting the 'formal - informal' distinction as one where 'authority is the *potentiality* to influence based on a position, whereas power is the actual ability of influence based on a number of factors including, of course, organizational position' (p.144).
     This definition of the topic becomes the basis for the mainstream of organization-theory studies of power.   The focus of investigation is defined in terms of deviations from the formal structure. This formal structure then appears in the analysis only in so far as it frames the initial state of rest, of equilibrium, from which the power deviation is to be measured.   In itself it is not a topic for investigation or explanation.   The topic becomes the *exercise* of power from within an initial equilibrium position, where that exercise is premised on the possession of some resource(s) by the power-holder.
     Defining the topic in this way has at least two important consequences.   First, it can lead to analyses of power which take the formal structure so much for granted that the author(s) frequently forget its existence in their zest to explicate the causal bases of power, as for instance Mechanic (1962), or Hickson et al. (1971).
     Mechanic (1962) proceeds from Weber's (1968) argument that permanent officials can frequently exercise power over elected representatives because such officials have a special knowledge due to their permanency vis-à-vis members elected for the life of a parliament.   He then extends this argument to all organizations. It is hardly legitimate to extend an argument concerned with representative government to all organizations in general.   It is certainly not legitimate to do so where the critical feature of the

original argument is missing.   This is the case where the executive is not elected on a precarious and revokable basis, compared to a permanent administrative staff.

Mechanic (1962) also displays another representative tendency in studies of 'power' which define it as the *exercise* of 'will' (Weber, 1947), or 'force' (Mechanic, 1962) or 'determination' (Thompson, 1956), or any similar formulation.   That is that this 'exercise' is premised on specific 'bases'.   These 'bases' have typically been conceptualized in one or other of two ways.   One of these can be characterized as 'functionalist' because the bases are sought in the 'functions' of the organizational system.   Examples of this can be seen in Thompson (1956) and Dubin (1957).

In a study of two USAF bomber wings Thompson (1956) argues that these 'bases' develop 'because of the technical requirements of operations' and suggests that they include being in a 'centralized' position within the organization, and being involved in strategic 'communication'.   Dubin (1957, p.62) similarly stresses 'the technical requirements of operations' with his emphasis on a 'system of functional interdependence' in which some tasks will be highly 'essential' to the system, and are the 'exclusive' function of a specific 'party'.

Bases of 'power' have also been sought in specific socially sanctioned 'resources' which the individual may control, or be in some special relationship with, such that they somehow enable 'power' to be 'exercised'.   A typical formulation would be that of French and Raven (1959) in which an a priori list of 'power resources' is constituted.   The problems with any such list, no matter what its constitution may be, are apparent.   Such an explanation assumes that the particular 'resources' which have a utility in one situation will have that utility in all situations.   It also assumes perfect knowledge on the part of all people in being able to judge correctly the utility of all resources in all situations.   Such assumptions are without warrant, and can only be guaranteed within the ideological practice of capitalist society, as Sensat and Constantine (1975) argue in their 'Critique of the Foundations of Utility Theory'.   Thus, explanations premised on this assumption presume that individual utilities of different 'resources' can be aggregated on a single measuring scale.   This is to deny changing historical circumstances, or different societal locales.   The assumption of 'resource'-based explanations of 'power' ought also to entail an exposition of how some people come to have access to these 'resources' while some others do not.   The prior possession of resources in anything other than equal amounts is something which a theory of 'power' has to explain.   It may presume equilibrium, but it ought to justify its presumption in some way. (3)

Organization theories of 'power' have not warranted this assumption of equilibrium.   They have presumed it.   This presumption consists of the simple expedient of taking the prior and inequitable distribution of resources for granted.   This is explicable when one considers the diachronic development of the meaning which was the language in use for theorizing about power in organizations, in particular from Thompson's (1956) article onwards.   A 'view' of 'power in organizations' developed as a study of variance or deviance from a presumedly unproblematic formal structure.   This then

became an immanent feature of an organization theory which has developed in an almost incestual conversation with its own voices - a
monologue, rather than a dialogue, and one which was conducted in
methodical insulation from the conversation of organizational life.

By the late 1960s there had developed a small literature on
'power in organizations'.   There existed a general consensus on a
concept of 'power' as an 'exercise' of 'will', 'determination',
etc., which was usually modelled upon Dahl's (1957) mechanical
model. (4)   The formal structure of hierarchical power in the organization was rarely discussed except in descriptive ways by writers
such as Tannenbaum (1968).   Increasingly the possible 'bases' of
'power' were modelled upon abstract concepts current in the literature, rather than specific social psychologists' lists.   The most
pervasive became Crozier's (1964) initially quite concrete concept
of 'uncertainty', control of which he had linked to 'power' (albeit
of a marginal and discretionary type).   The concept was in vogue.
It had become a mainstay of the 'Behavioural Theory of the Firm' as
Cyert and March (1963) modelled it.   It was at the centre of the
cybernetic and information-theory metaphors which pervaded organization theory in its search for the definitive system analogy, a
search which finds its most developed expression in Weick (1969),
who seems to point toward the ultimate telos of the metaphor in a
determinate physio-biology of the brain.   And the concept of
'uncertainty' which was implicit in Thompson's (1956) stress on
control of 'strategic communication' as a base of 'power' becomes
explicit in his 'Organizations in Action' (1967).

It was at this stage in the development of the language game
that a group of researchers led by Hickson attempted a 'synthesis'
of much of the available material, perhaps on the basis that with a
shopping list one might as well have a recipe.   They called their
recipe A Strategic Contingencies Theory of Intra-Organizational
Power (Hickson et al., 1971).

The 'strategic contingencies' theory of power is no exception in
theorizing from an initial assumption of equilibrium in the organization.   The theory does not do so within the terms of the initial
'informal - formal' dichotomy.   Because it is able to conceptualize
the organization outside of these terms it is able to abstract
entirely the formal structure of power out of the analysis.
Lawrence and Lorsch's (1967, p.3) re-definition of the organization
as 'a system of interrelated behaviours of people who are performing
a task that has been differentiated into several distinct sub-ystems
systems' provides the opportunity for this re-conceptualization.

The adoption of these premises leads to a theoretical equilibrium
achieved through a twofold abstraction.   First, it abstracts the
prior distribution of hierarchical power out of its 'picture'
through the familiar expedient of ignoring it.   The theory is able
to do this by conceptualizing the organization not as pyramidial
but as an 'interdepartmental system' after the manner of Lawrence
and Lorsch, in which 'the division of labour becomes the ultimate
source of intra-organizational power, and power is explained by
variables that are elements of each subunit's task, its functioning,
and its links with the activities of other subunits' (Hickson et
al., 1971, p.217).

The second abstraction is in not accounting for the fact that where 'sub-units' can be said to have engaged in 'the determination of behaviour' (Hickson et al., 1971, p.218), then this implies the prior power of the management of that sub-unit in being able to speak and act for sub-unit members.   Without this explication we are left with a reification in which the possibility of a sub-unit is never formulated.   There is no account of how the departmental management, rather than the work force, speak *for* the sub-unit, as a sub-unit of unitary and harmonious voices and views.   The possibilities of internal conflicts and fundamental clashes of interest are never raised.   That these differences count for nothing, and are rarely aired by the management of the sub-unit, merely reaffirms the pyramidial power structure of the organization, rather than suppresses it.   The 'power' of the sub-unit has to be grounded in the prior *capacity* to exercise power which managers possess. And they do not possess this because of the interactions of variables which entitle one sub-unit to more bases of 'power' than the others, except in the likely stories of organization theory.   The variables which will measure this 'power' (Hinings et al., 1974) are an aggregation culled from the diachrony of the language game (Hickson et al., 1971).   Hence we find that 'power' is equivalent to being 'central', 'unsubstitutable', in 'control' of 'uncertainty', etc.   The theory has no account of why a particular type of inter-relationship should dispose sub-units to *exercise* 'power', or, to de-reify the theory, why these should dispose particular managers to *exercise* 'power'.   All it provides is an implicit assumption that there exists such a craving for 'power' that anyone who has the chance to exercise it will do so. (5)

One of the most surprising features of the previously cited literature is the way it has developed in isolation from the lively community power debate in political science.   One consequence of this has been the uncritical application of a concept of 'power' which has been subject to extensive criticism.   I refer to the critique of Dahl's (1957) concept of 'power' by writers such as Bachrach and Baratz (1962, 1971).   One writer on The Role of 'power' in Organization Theory who has addressed this literature is Abell (1975).

Abell (1975) attempts to circumvent three particular problems in his discussion of 'power'.   First, he attempts to break with the tradition which he terms the 'control of resources' approach (ibid., p.1).   Second, he proposes to study 'decision making' (6) rather than rely on a 'reputational approach' (7) to data collection (ibid.).   Third, he proposes a two-stage model of the organization as a 'bargaining and influence system' in which it is proposed to incorporate Bachrach and Baratz's (1962) argument that 'what is and what is not open to bargaining is itself related to the concept of power' (Abell, 1975, p.1).

Abell (op. cit., p.3) rejects the use of 'resources' or 'bases' as an 'operational definition' of 'power' (on grounds similar to those I have employed earlier).   Instead he proposes that one should first detect the 'power' or 'influence' of a group or person, and then provide an explanation of this power in terms of resources. The distinction between 'power' and 'influence' that Abell makes is quite specific, and serves the purpose of attempting to incorporate Bachrach and Baratz's (1962) critique of Dahl's concept of 'power' into organizational analysis.

The crux of Bachrach and Baratz's (1962) critique lies in the proposition that the study of 'power' should be extended to a study of 'non-decisions' as well as decisions, and to a study of the 'mobilization of bias' (Schattschneider, 1960) as it is embodied in dominant values, political myths, rituals and institutions which customarily rule in some issues while some others are just as routinely ruled out.

Abell (1975, p.5) argues that if we can obtain data on people's 'initial preferred outcomes' to a decision, and observe the 'ability of A to modify B's preferred outcomes in a bargaining/influence situation all other influences "held constant" then this will give us the influence of A over B in securing B's "modified preferred outcomes"'.   The 'bargaining power' of A will then be 'his ability to obtain his preferred outcomes, when facing competing preferred outcomes, in a bargaining situation, all other bargaining power held constant', determined by the 'final bargained outcome'.   But although this approach does not simply aggregate 'bases' or 'resources' and does not depend on a simple assumption of an initial equilibrium, it is still not really satisfactory.   The 'initial preferred outcomes' that people will have are in a sense arbitrary. They will depend upon *when* the researcher has defined the bargaining sequence as beginning.   Nor is an 'initial preferred outcome' as unproblematic as it might at first sight seem to be.   What constitutes an 'initial preferred outcome' may be the very problem that we wish to address, rather than its solution.   To the extent that a person's theorizing of the possibilities of their existence and participation in an organization will be circumscribed within the dominant theorizing power of the organization's form of life, then surely a very significant form of power will be the members' inability to see beyond the actuality of presence?   In Marcuse's (1964) phrase, they will be one-dimensional men embedded within the unthought consensus of everyday life.

III

The one-dimensionality of organizational life depicted as a textual feature of organization theory ironically mirrors the organization of these organization texts.   One can read any one text as standing for any other, despite that each seeks to say something extra, more cumulative, additional or novel in comparison with preceding texts. These seeming differences are rooted in the notion which can produce Other, and other texts as something to be superseded, added to, or made redundant.   The differences of the texts, the variables deployed, the arguments used, these are only explicable as moves in a language game whose implicit differences are rooted in the deep sameness of one tradition of discourse, that of positive, positivist speaking and writing.

This goes some way to explaining my argument thus far.   If my text is not simply to be a counter-move in the same language game in which I propose something extra in the way of variables, or something different in their inter-relations, then I must constitute these preceding texts not as Other, as something other to, and prior to myself, and my own writing.   I cannot simply 'view' them

passively as organization theory would have it done.   Only that
which is most obvious and apparent, such as an outcome to a decision
(a text as a definition which defines itself), is on 'view'.   What
is not viewable is that which the viewed covers over.   Just as we
should not be content to accept concrete decision-making as the
display of power, then we ought not to be content to accept the
stipulations of definition (the way the text defines itself) as the
display of theorizing power.   The texts of organization theory do
not constitute others (for me) to be superseded or underlaboured at.
They serve as reminders of the way our craft exemplifies Otherness -
an exemplification which invites intervention, dispersal and remembrance - remembrance of its suppressed history of silence.

This silence can be shown through locating organization theories
of power within a broader tradition of writing on the topic.   In
doing this we find that the concept of power has been thought in
two quite distinct yet related ways.   Each of these proposes a
distinct theorizing (of) power, one of which is formulated after a
relatively recent ontology, the older of which goes back at least
as far as Plato.   The distinctions between them can elaborate the
metaphors of organization theory.   The connections between them
can propose a social theory of that topic which organization theory
has defined as 'power'.

IV

If one knew nothing of organizations in our contemporary capitalist
society, yet one was willing to absorb what knowledge one could
from the existing scholarly texts on the topic, what picture of
power would these present?

One might be led to think that organizations were composed of
'behaviours' (Lawrence and Lorsch, 1967, p.3) which belonged to
something called a 'sub-unit' which occupied a space in a 'system'
(Hickson et al., 1971, p.217).   These sub-units are engaged in a
permanent struggle with each other as each tries to control more
aggregated 'bases' of 'power' than the others (Butler et al., 1974;
Hickson et al., 1971).   Sometimes these behaviours and sub-units
form 'coalitions' with others of their kind, from inside or outside
the same system.   Coalitions are usually not very stable, and
change over specific issues (Benson, 1975; Butler et al., 1974).

As with much science fiction which features alien beings one
finds no explanation of the Hobbesian assumptions.   Sub-units, like
Daleks, just happen to be like that.   And if we recognize human
beings inside the Dalek shell, or inside the sub-unit - well, it
must just be that it is somehow *in* human nature to strive for power
like that.   None of our scholars tells us otherwise.

The assumption of a 'power struggle' as a principle of the system
fulfils the same function in organization theory as does the principle of unfettered competition in economic models of price equilibrium (after Macpherson, 1973, pp.184-91).   These economic models
are premised on the assumption of a freely competitive market for
resources and commodities in which there exists a division of labour
and exchange of products and labour.   It is assumed that each individual in this market would rationally try to maximize his or her

gains (or minimize the real costs).   Where both a division of
labour and an exchange of commodities and labour exist, then it
would follow that competition would determine prices for everything
in a determinate system which tended to equilibrium (as Lipsey,
1963, demonstrates).

Organization theory rephrases these assumptions but without substantially altering the problematic of 'equilibrium' which they
animate.   In organization theory the equilibrium is achieved
through the creation of 'dependencies'.

On the assumption of a freely competitive power struggle in the
organization's market (its 'bargaining zone' in Abell's phrase), in
which, as in economic theory, each individual tried to maximize his
or her gains (or minimize the real costs), where the division of
labour creates exchanges, then it would follow that control of
scarce 'resources' or 'bases' of exchange, would maximize dependencies for everyone (as in Hickson et al., 1971).   And, where
'power' is defined as the obverse of 'dependency' then we would have
achieved a theory of power in a determinate system which tended to
equilibrium as in economics - or in organization theory as Hickson
et al. (1971) render it.

Such a model is premised on a market model whose motive force is
a series of ontological assumptions about Being:

to treat the maximization of utilities as the ultimate justification of a society, is to view man as essentially a consumer of
utilities.   It is only when man is seen as essentially a bundle
of appetites demanding satisfaction that the good society is
the one which maximizes satisfactions (Macpherson, 1973, p.4).

This is a distinctively different concept of Being from that
which is found in the tradition of political theory as it is seen
in Plato's 'Republic' for instance.   Here the good society is that
in which men are free to use and develop their natural abilities,
attributes and capacities.   In this version of 'power', for it to
be exercised, the person must have access to whatever means are
necessary in order that he or she may use and develop their natural
attributes, capacities and abilities.   To the extent that this
access is denied, or limited and transferred to others, this 'power'
is diminished (Macpherson, 1962, p.56).   This conception of Being
leads to a quite different concept of 'power' from that which has
previously been sketched.   While the obverse of Being exercising
'power' in these formulations may be Being 'dependent', in the older
formulations Being 'free' is opposed to Being under 'power'.

Adopting this latter view has some important consequences for our
theorizing.   It concentrates our thought on the theoretically and
practically prior conditions for the 'exercise' of 'power'.   The
essence of this view of 'power' is to see it as 'potential' or
'capacity' for future action, *including any specific exercise of
'power'*.   In ordinary language, it would be the type of 'power'
meant when we say that someone 'has power', or when we speak of
someone 'being in power'.

To abstract this latter concept is to distract our attention from
the underlying social relations that grant to some positions in
organizations more or less 'capacity' to 'exercise' power than
others.   Instead it focuses our attention on the 'exercise' after
any prior structuring of 'capacity' has occurred.   'Power' is seen

simply as the 'exercise' of an 'ability', *taken after any accretion or diminution of 'capacity' has occurred*.

This concept of 'power' does not stipulate access to whatever means are neccessary to *exercise* this capacity; instead it abstracts the whole question of 'capacity' out of consideration. 'Power' is power over others only after some 'exercise' moves the state of play from some point *taken* as an initial state of rest. There is no specification of how the rules of play have developed, nor of how they might grant a greater 'capacity' to one set of players, over the others.   This has the ideological function of preserving the structural framework of social relations as something outside, and prior to, theoretical enquiry into 'power'.   *Thus this structural framework cannot enter into any explanation of how the 'exercise' of power can create a 'variance' from 'authority'.*

The remainder of the argument seeks to open a space whereby this may be possible.

Organization theory re-presents the ontological assumptions of the market theory which developed as a justification for liberal-democratic society from Hobbes onwards (and is still being developed by contemporary theorists of the right).   Marx came to refer to its economic doctrine as 'vulgar' political economy.   One might refer, after the same manner, to 'vulgar' organization theory.   Rowthorn (1974) has detailed the ontological assumptions of vulgar political economy as *subjective individualism, naturalism* and *exchange*.   By showing how these premise vulgar organization theory, much as they do vulgar political economy, it is possible to suggest an alternative way of seeing organizations which enables us to provide a basis for connecting discussion of 'power' with that of 'domination' and 'autonomy'.

I have discussed the subjective individualism of organization theories whose seemingly structural concepts such as a sub-unit have to be regarded as being premised, methodologically, on individual manager's 'power'.   Although Weber is also frequently castigated for being 'methodologically individualist' in his concept of 'power' (for instance, Lukes, 1974), this is only correctly observed if one chooses not to consider the context in which Weber (1968) developed his concern with 'power'.   Thus, if one compares the individuals premised in organization theories with those premised by Weber (1968) in his writings on 'power, rule and domination', one may find there a truly social conception of human motivation, rather than one premised on either the metaphysics of Hobbes or uncertainty-reduction.

For Weber (1968) individual social actions are not motivated either by an insatiable desire for power or for certainty, but by collectively recognized and publicly available social rules which orient individual social actions in rationally structured ways.   He notes that these rules, in so far as they 'form' social actions are 'without exception ... profoundly influenced by structures of dominancy' (Weber, 1968, p.941), which do not

> utilize in every case economic power for (their) foundation and maintenance.   But in the vast majority of cases, and indeed in the most important ones, this is just what happens in one way or another and often to such an extent that the mode of applying economic means for the purpose of maintaining domination, in

turn exercises a determining influence on the structure of dominancy.   The crucial characteristics of any form of domination, may it is true, not be correlated in any clearcut fashion with any particular form of economic organization.   Yet the structure of dominancy is in many cases both a factor of great economic importance and at least to some extent a result of economic conditions (Weber, 1968, p.942).

'Power' as a particular type of social action is constructed and acted out by individuals as a ruled enactment.   Such enactments occur in the context of an economically conditioned structure of domination.   The individual is a 'bearer' of a particular rationality in which an 'objective principle' is regarded as a 'concrete object' which 'governs the domination', as Simmel (1971, p.116) put it (also see Clegg, 1975, pp.63-5).   The individual is essentially a social being, who, as a bearer of social relations, is ruled and dominated in the last instance by economic power.   This economic power is embedded and displayed within the framework of a 'structure of domination' which is articulated through different types of 'rule'.   Domination thus concerns, and grants, the prior capacity to be able to 'exercise' power at all.

There is no room in such a sociology for the *naturalist* and *ahistorical* tendencies that find their expression in current versions of the organization as a natural system.   Contrary to this view is one which poses an understanding of the organization as the locus of the domination of a specific form of life. (8)   This is that of the juncture of materials with ideas about the relationship of these to each other.   These materials comprise not only the organization's site, plant, capital and raw materials, but also its labour.   Within organizations constituted under a capitalist form of life it is the case that this labour is also regarded descriptively as just another commodity to be exploited (Macpherson, 1973, p.10).   The basis of the organization is the 'labour-power' (Marx, 1973, p.154), the 'capacity for labour' of the individuals who collectively comprise the creativity of the organization.   Some of these members control not only their own creativity, their own 'capacity for labour', but also that of other members through the formal distribution of domination.   Those members who have less than full control of their labour power will have a consequently limited capacity to exercise power because of their relative loss of freedom.

This implies a different perspective on 'membership' from that which is typically found in such organization theory formulations as those of March and Simon (1958) or Barnard (1966).   These stress the conditions under which human and material resources *exchange* for one another, and formulate these in terms of 'inducements' and 'contributions'.   If an exchange occurs the theory proposes that it must be a fair exchange because each person involved in the exchange must have weighed up their inducements and contributions so that they subjectively balance, or are in equilibrium for the induced party.   Otherwise an exchange would not have occurred. This neglects that a seemingly fair exchange may be underlain by a prior structure of relations which make inevitable an exchange based on a set of terms which as a rule favour the interests of one party above that of the other(s).   It is in this way that Marx

(1973) analyses the relations between Labour and Capital.   This
analysis proposes a theoretical understanding of the *social* relations which are entered into in organized employment and production.
   Marx (1973) argues that what the worker sells to the capitalist
in return for his wages is his labour power.   Marx maintains that
this cannot be a fair exchange.   If it were, the capitalist would
quickly have no money left.   This would be because if the capitalist did not share in the labour then all the money would soon
pass to the labourer.   Where there existed profit there could be
no fair exchange. (9)   What might appear on the surface to be a
just exchange 'inducing' the 'contribution' of organizational membership will in fact have to be an unjust and exploitative exchange
if the organization as the capitalist's instrument for materializing
profit is to remain in being in the long run. (10)   Exploitation
concerns the way in which under the institution of the market the
capacity concept of power is organized as a form of domination which
provides the framework within which power may be exercised.   In
capitalist organizations exploitation is the material basis of
Capital's domination of Labour as a class (as Cole's introduction
to Marx (1957) reiterates concisely).   Capital, and its functionaries in management (between whom Marx (1962, p.427) argues that no
distinction be made), has a greater prior capacity for an exercise
of power because its very existence is premised on the diminution
of the power of Labour (also see Macpherson, 1973, pp.43-5).
   Profit, or surplus value minus costs, which Marx (1973, pp.194-
207) defines as those of constant and variable capital, is the
organization standard whereby the creativity of current labour and
the determinations of past labours are mediated.   Current labour
is organized around the organization's location in a mode of production and the strategies by which surplus value is to be accumulated, be it through either absolute, relative or indirect accumulation (see O'Connor, 1974).   The relative profitability of each
of these strategies will depend upon the juncture of the organization's location in a mode of production and the past history
it represents, with the current costs of commodities, including
labour, and the present possibilities of the world economy as a
superstructure.
   Power has been typically formulated as a variance from formal
structure in organization theory.   This version of 'power' is still
in need of explanation even if one rejects current attempts at such
explanations.   Discrediting the explanations does not always remove
the problem to be explained.   How might a variance from the formal
structure of domination within an organization be achieved?
   Variances from a formal structure of domination might be explained by means of a model which affords a mediation between the
different levels of structures.   Let us consider the structure of
the world capitalist economy as a social formation.   The concept
of stages of development of surplus value accumulation enables us
to do that.   For Capital, the world is a multitude of arenas
awaiting profitable exploitation.   Chance and history may combine
to present one or other arena as particularly favourable for Capital
to produce in at any given moment.   This will be determined by the
particular choice of the organization's executives in their analysis
of the possibilities of accumulating surplus value from the arena's

'commodities'.   These commodities may include factors such as com-
pliant government or unions, political stability, favourable exchange rates or tax laws, availability of resources of labour, raw
materials, technology, capital, etc.   Any organization's lists of
any arena's possible 'commodities' will depend upon its relationship
to the stages of development of surplus value accumulation strategies, and the extent to which the organization is typified by being
either a Merchant, Industrial or Technological Capitalist (Karpik,
1972).   Obviously a firm dealing in the accumulation of absolute
surplus value in a local product market would not realistically
consider moving its plant to an area of lower-cost labour.   But it
might decide to import this lower-cost labour into its organization,
as has been the historical tendency in the construction industry
(recently documented in its contemporary European aspect by John
Berger (1975)).

This mediation may be analysed further by using the concept of
'modes of rationality', a concept similar to that which Lucien
Karpik (1972) termed 'logics of action'.   This affords a mediation
between the totality of structures, the specific organization, and
the specific exercise of power.

The ideal of capitalist practice, the materialization of 'profitability' as an icon, an ideal of practice (the reality of which
the research of Pahl and Winkler (1974, p.118) re-affirms), co-
exists as an objective principle with different modes of rationality
for achieving the production of our material life.   This material
life will concern the application of specific techniques, and technologies to the materialization of this ideal.   It can give us
such categories as shipbuilding, mining, construction, insurance,
or techniques such as asset-stripping.

The material life of the organization may be classified in terms
of its modes of rationality: these are the strategies and tactics
by which the organization's executive orient towards the accumulation of surplus value in their pursuit of the ideal of profitability, and its materialization.   At any one time any one or more
of these may have a decisive role in the corporate strategy of the
organization.   Many such modes of rationality are theoretically
possible, but in any actual case they will to some extent be limited
by the particular material life under consideration.   The particular mode(s) of rationality of the organization will be a result
of past interaction between the particular material life, and the
requirements of a wider economic framework, the juxtaposition of
choices in technology and choices in markets with the organization's
location at a particular stage of capitalist development.   These
past choices will have involved specific policy decisions (possibly
constructed as reactions to 'market forces'), which will have
entailed a variable commitment of organizational resources, thus
incurring for management more or less reversible 'management for
objectives'.   The particular mode(s) of rationality of a given
organization have to be constructed by the researcher out of whatever available empirical materials and 'social traces' (such as
company documents, financial records, advertisements, tape record-
ings of executive meetings, etc.) are available to him.

Weber's (1968, p.942) discussion of 'domination' and 'influence'
may now be re-instituted in relation to the concept of mode(s) of
rationality.

Weber (1968, p.942) has stressed that 'the mode of applying economic means for the purpose of maintaining domination ... exercises a determining *influence* on the structure of domination' (italics mine).   This remark suggests a theoretical understanding of the topic which organization theory has constituted as 'power in organizations', which, as I have elaborated, concerns the explanation of variance (where it exists) from the formal structure of domination within the organization.

Weber regards this as a problem of explaining 'influence' rather than 'power'.   A theory of the 'exercise' of 'a determining influence on the structure of domination' would have to provide an explanation of how certain types of exercise of power enable the power-wielders to become incorporated into the formal structure of domination in the organization.

Given that power, when it is exercised, is exerted over 'issues', then the crucial point would be to determine which issues are critical for the organization (which implies the corollaries of non-criticality and non-issues).   Once we have determined what these are, we can establish which management function(s) are responsible for the domain in which they occur.   I suggest that a critical issue will be one which effects the ideal of profitability as it is manifested in the organization's mode(s) of rationality.   As Pahl and Winkler (1974, p.115) put it, 'In a capitalist society, effective economic power lies with those who have the ability to conceive and carry through schemes for the profitable allocation of capital'.

The major exercise of formally warranted power in the organization (because it is generated by members orienting themselves to the iconic domination of the ideal of profitability) will concern issues that effect the rational functioning of this means of accumulating and appropriating surplus value.   That is, power will be exercised to re-assert control.   Thus, power relations are only the visible tip of a structure of control, rule and domination which maintains its effectiveness not so much through overt action, as through its ability to appear to be *the* natural convention.   It is only when taken-for-grantedness fails, routines lapse, and 'problems' appear, that the overt exercise of power is necessary.   And this is exerted to re-assert control.   This control is ultimately measured in financial terms such as 'profit', 'growth', and 'return on investments'.

If we were to have a theory of 'significant issues' in the organization, we would implicitly have a theory concerning the functioning of power.   The position(s) that exercised power over 'significant issues' would then be the positions that had the effective functioning power to act on issues.   They would be able to do this only within the framework of domination to whose icon they would first have to submit - the possibility of an issue would have to be framed within its theorizing power for it to be ruled admissible. (11)

Where the formal structure of domination within the organization and the functioning of power no longer cohere, as a result of the historical development of the organization, then we would anticipate that unless contradictions persist unchecked - which they very well might - a political process of incorporation into the structure of the organization would be in process, whereby this coherence would

be re-established.   In this way the administrative functioning of
power within the executive's formally conceived structure of domination develops as a dynamic, processual response to strategic
changes within the organization.   These changes are constructed by
the executive as the organization's response to the exploitative
possibilities inherent in the process of the uneven developments of
the means of accumulating surplus value. (12)

While the rationality of this domination in its 'routine' (13)
and its 'rule' and the issues that it enables is sociologically
interesting, and ethnomethodologically researchable, the fortunes
of the particular individuals who are tied up with these are not.
But their rise and fall in the managerial pecking order can serve
to display the movement and contradictions of capitalist development
at a particular place and time.   I have suggested that it is to
the history of these contradictions that a theory of the functioning
of power in organizations might look.

A theory of influence, of the functioning of power under Capital,
could locate an explanation of power variance from the formal structure of domination in terms of contradictions wrought in the organization by virtue of its past history and present being.   Its past
history, representing the conditions under which its members now
labour, and the specific social relations into which they enter
presents the organization members with a limited number of strategies by which to assert their current labour.   This labour is limited by the dead weight of the past, in terms of past investment,
production, research, marketing and accounting decisions.   This
organizational history constructs an arena and a structure of rules
around which negotiations can develop.

V

The theme that I have proposed as being typified by the idea of
'organizational history' can serve not only to depict the concrete
possibilities of any organization as a topic, it can also be used
reflexively to re-view the organization theory that I have reviewed.

Organization theory, its labour limited by the dead weight of
past investment, production, research, marketing and accounting
decisions, not surprisingly choses to follow the theorizing it does
given the massive investments of past labour expended in formulating
and following conventional modes of discourse. They represent its
'intellectual capital' (Bourdieu, 1975).

As Marx put it in the oft-quoted phrase from the 'Eighteenth
Brumaire of Louis Bonaparte':

   Men make their own history, but they do not make it just as they
   please; they do not make it under circumstances chosen by themselves, but under circumstances directly encountered, given and
   transmitted from the past. The tradition of all the dead gener-
   ations weighs like a nightmare on the brain of the living.
   And just when they seem engaged in revolutionizing themselves
   and things, and creating something that has never yet existed,
   precisely in such periods of revolutionary crisis they anxiously
   conjure up the spirits of the past to their service and borrow
   from them names, battle cries, and costumes in order to present

the new scene of world history in this time-honoured disguise
and this borrowed language (Marx, 1969, p.360).

One always has to 'borrow' language.   This does not mean that
one is condemned to the same meaning as the use of the language in
the context from which one borrows.   Given time and material transformation, meaning may undergo significant shifts - shifts which
can occur only through a speaking which in interrupting has to speak
to and *with* its chosen discourse.   And this discourse, in so far as
it represents the accumulated theoretical capital of all the past
ages, cannot be ignored - it must be confronted in a rational discourse which engages the tradition it seeks to transform. (14)
Anything other than a commitment to positive dialectics would be a
merely nihilistic outburst, an act of purely emotional rather than
political passion.

Yet the engagement itself cannot stand for Reason.   Through no
choice of one's self one may yet be condemned to nihilism.   Reason
demands a response which may not be forthcoming.   As Pierre Bourdieu
(1975, p.17) has put it: 'As accumulated scientific resources
increase, so the incorporated scientific capital needed in order to
appropriate them and thereby gain access to scientific problems and
tools, and thus to the scientific struggle, becomes greater (the
costs of entry).'

One consequence of the skirmishes that I have conducted herein
(as a guerrilla sniping at an established order) may be the condem-
nation of my own analysis to silence in the reluctance of the cus-
todians of intellectual capital to engage in what might be the
involuntary liquidation of their intellectual investments.   Thus
the importance of speaking through the borrowed language - one is
obliged to do so in order to stake a claim to legitimacy, in order
to be taken 'seriously' (see Silverman, 1974), with all the risks
of 'anxiously conjuring up ... spirits of the past' which this use
of a pre-empted language entails.

In conclusion, I will consider to what extent it is possible that
one can create an alternative social production - theory - through
the existing 'borrowed language'.   I have suggested that two concepts of power are necessary for an analysis of power in organizations.   Conventionally, only one of these is found in organization
theory.   This is a concern with the 'exercise' of 'power' as a
variance from a formal structure of domination.   Domination concerns the second concept of power.   This stresses the notion of
'capacity'.   I then went on to suggest that the two types of power
may be seen to relate to underlying ontologies.   The more recent
of these developed as part of the liberal-democratic justificatory
theory for market society.   This version stresses the 'exercise'
of power.   I suggested that it could be seen to underpin organization theorists' conceptions of power.   In this context it has
had a definite ideological function by suppressing the 'capacity'
concept of power.   It abstracts our attention away from the social
relations of production which undergird power.   It proposes
theories whose end result is a mystification of these relations in
the metaphors of 'uncertainty'.

The same assumptions that underlie 'vulgar' political economy,
derived from the general liberal-democratic theory, also gird what
we might call 'vulgar' organization theory.   A critique of this

'vulgar science' can be opposed to present organization theories of power in order to institute the possibility of a social theory. Such a theory is grounded in an understanding of the organization as a mediation of structures and material and ideal factors. The concept of the ideal of profitability serves as the synthesis between the social structure of capitalism in the process of uneven development, and the organization members as functionaries responsible for executing the organization's 'mode of rationality'. Being in the position of administering the mode of rationality grants the manager(s) concerned the 'potential' to exercise 'influence' upon strategic and policy decision-making. Where this management is not incorporated into the formal structure of domination within the organization, then contradictions may emerge between the authorized structure of domination and its functioning. These contradictions may or may not be resolved by the re-negotiation of the function in question within the formal structure. To the extent that organization theories of 'power' deal with this phenomenom of variance in the formal structure they may be more correctly characterized as theories of 'influence' as Weber (1968) noted.

A theory of power in the organization *over and above the existing structure of domination* could only arise against Capital, rather than *for* Capital. As long as the theorizing power of Capital holds ideological sway over the possibilities of membership this is unlikely to emerge. To the extent that practice is informed by theory, theory which suggests that a change of faces, a change of influence, is a change in power is theory which serves the interests of those, and that, which has power. It is theorizing for Capital.

In seeking to oppose the conceptual 'exercise' of power in organization theory through re-opening this theory to the conceptual 'capacity' of power, it was inevitable that this should find me seeking to exert power. This must always be a corollary of any action exerted to appropriate a means of production. What I have sought to do in this paper is to make it essential that such a positive appropriation should not serve merely to re-present the silence of speech which is ignorant of itself, because it is in such ignorance that the historical rootedness of any speech is forgotten, and present Being taken as a suppression of future Becoming. I put it to you that if our organization theory is to have any relevance for our liberation from existing forms of domination, then it must begin by offering the basis for a theoretical understanding of this domination. If this possibility could be opened, then might organizations and organization theory be interrupted.

NOTES

Thanks are due to David Dunkerley, David Silverman and Brian Torode for helpful comments and criticisms on the paper during its genesis. In addition, I would also like to thank the members of seminars in Bradford, London, Paris and Berlin, who commented on it in various stages of its preparation.
  1 I take this point of Gramsci's to be similar to arguments which
     stress that theory ought to account both for its own production
     and the production of that phenomenon which it addresses. Where

this is theory which has been constructed 'in ignorance of itself' criticism will involve the confrontation of the political significance of an intellectual practice with the way in which it is formulated.   These ideas are developed at greater length in Clegg (1976).   The frequent self-referencing in these notes should be read as a form of shorthand whereby the text may be contained while the reader is dispersed into other texts animated by similar concerns.   Generally these notes contain points of information and asides on the main body of the text.

2   The vexed issue of just how one might translate Weber (1968) on *macht* and *herrschaft* is discussed at greater length in Clegg (1975).

3   Arthur McCullough first made me aware of these issues during the many discussions that we had when colleagues at Bradford University.

4   Dahl's work is discussed in more detail in Clegg (1975) and also in Lukes (1974).

5   This is rather akin to a certain type of political analysis which argues against dependence upon any organized sector of the working class, such as dockers or miners, who are capable of controlling the distribution of some vital commodity or service.   What this version of the argument misses is that the infrequency of such 'disruptions' of 'everyday life' as the mineworkers' strike of 1974 is the measure of the domination of Capital over Labour, and the extent to which the theorizing power of the latter is so often constituted in the interests of the former.   Exercises of power are merely the surface expression of a much deeper domination.   This example is doubly illuminative, for it demonstrates that for the strategic contingencies theory to be applicable, there must be a sense of joint purpose and common organization in a collectivity organized *for* itself.   While a collectivity may act collectively *for* itself where the agents have a commonly realized class interest, such as where Labour defines itself against Capital, one would not anticipate that this consciousness would be as pervasive a feature where the agents in question are a branch of management. Management struggles tend to be internecine, rather than be waged on a common collective basis.   This suggests that the application of the strategic contingencies theory at the level of Labour-Capital/Union-Management relations which focus on the shop floor collectivity may be more realistic.   Marchington (1975a, 1975b) is currently engaged in research into this application.

6   The 'decision-making' approach to the study of power entails researching a number of *key decisions* covering a number of *issue-areas*.   Those who successfully initiate or oppose key decisions are then regarded as the most powerful members of the setting under review.

7   The 'reputational approach' to the study of power consists of asking people designated as *well-placed* or *well-informed* to compile a list of the *most influential people* according to their estimate of their *reputation* within the setting under review.

8   In proposing an understanding of organizational life which is

not premised on the specific variables constituted-as-properties
-of-the-organization of organization theory, then I am instead
proposing orienting towards an understanding of the organization
as a re-presentation of the institutions which gird our lives,
notably the institutions of the capitalist market.   Thus, it
should be clear that although the formal (form of the) analysis
may be employed across a wide number of institutional settings,
the specific content deployed here refers only to this most
pervasive icon of the market.

9   As Marx (1973, pp.321,322) put it: 'The surplus value which
capital has at the end of the productive process ... signifies
... that the labour time objectified in the product ... is
greater than that which was present in the original components
of capital.   This in turn is possible only if the labour objectified in the price of labour is smaller than the living labour
time purchased with it.'   Raw material and machinery represent
fixed amounts of objectified labour time as components of capital.   Where the price for labour, the wage, is exactly equal
in labour time payments to the amount of labour time the labourer has added to raw material and machinery,

then the capitalist would merely have exchanged exchange
value in one form for exchange value in another.   He would
not have acted as capital ... as far as the capitalist is
concerned, it has to be a not exchange.   He has to obtain
more value than he gives.   Looked at from the capitalists'
side, the exchange must be only *apparent*;   i.e. must belong
to an economic category other than exchange, or capital as
capital and labour as labour in opposition to it would be
impossible.

10 Such a statement presumes the following specifications.   First,
that capitalist society is one in which workers 'own' only their
'labour-power', or capacity for labour, while the capitalists
own all the means of production, the wage fund for labourers,
and scarce land.   This capacity for labour is regarded as a
commodity which, when used in the production process along with
the instruments and subjects of production (land and raw materials, Marx, 1954, ch. 7, section 2, cited in Bose, 1975, p.76)
produces surplus value which is appropriated by the capitalist.
This appropriation represents *exploitation* (not only in a moral
sense) because it involves control of one (class of) person(s)
by another.   In the long run exploitation exists wherever there
is this control (Crocker, 1973), not only where there is positive surplus value (Bose, 1975).

11 Alternative means of formulating issues might be through radical
action which openly challenges the dominant theorizing power.

12 At this juncture in reading or hearing this paper, two of my
colleagues in sociology said much the same thing to me - that I
would find few people in sociology who would disagree with this
analysis.   Good - I am not peddling novelty - but if this is the
case then is it not surprising that organization theory conjures
the analyses it does?   (Well, no, it's not surprising - but read
on!)

13 Parry and Morriss (1974) also stress the importance of 'routines' in the study of power.

14 On the question of what constitutes a 'rational discourse' see
Clegg (1976).

Chapter 4

TECHNOLOGICAL CAPITALISM

Lucien Karpik

SUMMARY

The analysis of the politics of large industrial enterprise encounters several difficulties: the knowledge of the universe of possible strategic choices; the revealing of the connections between
the global activity of the enterprise and that of the groups that
compose it; and the margin of autonomy of the firm. An attempt at
a solution is presented here. It is in fact possible to classify
the objectives of the enterprise according to the forms of ration-
alities or logics of action (logiques d'action); to identify for
large technological enterprise its specific restraints and the
methods of action at its disposal; and finally, to explain the
hierarchies of politics/logics of action by certain general deter-
minants.

Modern industrial societies, with the remnants and ruins inherited
from the past, those realities which are still living although they
were born in distant ages, the categories of phenomena which have
not yet reached historical maturity and which are juxtaposed with
others still being formed, constitute compositions which are so
diverse and contradictory, so rapid and abrupt in their evolution,
that an initial investigation does not bring out any apparent coherence either partial or general.
    While it is the role of sociology to discover an order which is
only that of its own theory, sociology cannot do this unless it
adopts various forms of reductionism. It does this by isolating
social facts from the historical situation. Consequently it
encounters as its first requirement the construction of a theory of
historical situations. This requirement, which was first formulated in France in the 1950s by a criticism of sociological empiri-
cism and formalism, and then imposed by the historical reactivation
of western societies, has engendered an extreme diversity of interpretations, many of which can be classified in two distinct series:
first, those which are based upon nineteenth-century prophecies,
the present utopias, the observations of social crisis or disorgan-
ization, and which have as a common reference a normative definition
of the 'good society'; second, those which accumulate propositions

starting from quantitative relationships between concrete phenomena
in the hope of achieving the general theory.

In order to resist the two temptations of the philosophy of
history and of positivism, this essay makes the methodological decision to envisage social facts as expressions of coherent and singu-
lar wholes, which are defined by specific rules of organization and
operation. Analysis of the most advanced form of economy can only
begin to examine the originality of its manifestations, and the
diversity of ways in which it is determined, by the construction
of a socio-historical theory, however partial and provisional it
may be.

This paper is devoted exclusively to the *production of material
life* and more precisely to its most evolved mode which I shall refer
to as 'technological capitalism'. Without going into the discussions which this formulation may engender, I define the economic
as the system of relationships between production, exchange and consumption of goods and services whose prices are directly or indirectly fixed by market forces, and, consequently, I establish the
characteristics which, in their general or particular forms, enable
us by examining their variations, to make a reasoned comparison of
economic systems.

For the period of 'industrial civilization', a phrase borrowed
from A. Touraine, it is possible to distinguish three pure economic
forms whose importance varies at different periods of history and
within different branches of production: 'merchant capitalism'
characterizes England at the time of the Poor Laws and then progressively the other countries of Western Europe, achieving its
highest form in the second half of the nineteenth century and then
declining in the more industrialized societies; 'industrial capitalism' manifests itself more fully in the 1950s, in particular in
the mass-production sectors; and 'technological capitalism' appears
progressively in the 'technologically advanced' industries from the
1960s.

A presentation of 'merchant capitalism' and 'industrial capitalism' ought by comparison to enable us to define that which is
original in 'technological capitalism'. One would nevertheless
have to define the conditions and limits. First, this classification is not the only possible one and the arbitrary choice directly expresses the theoretical question with which we are concerned, namely the explanation of economic evolution as a function
of the relationship between the combination of knowledge and industry, and social relationships. Second, if it is true that private
ownership of the means of production does not intervene as a distinguishing criterion, this is because the actual holding by a
social minority is a characteristic common to all forms of economy
in industrial civilization. Third, this analysis will necessarily
be very schematic and its interest can only be retrospective; it
is to the extent that the interpretation of 'technological capitalism' is convincing that it may justify a systematic analysis of
other forms of economy.

'Merchant capitalism' is by definition dominated by a new mode
of economic organization: the market, unknown by previous societies
in which the seeking of profit was not the legitimate end of human
activities and in which the economic system was subordinated to

social and religious requirements.   It was in England at the end of
the eighteenth century that merchant economy began in its full and
rigorous form: all goods and all resources derived from the market.

In this society, for the first time, work and nature are assimilated to merchandise.   The price mechanism becomes the basis of the
table of equivalences which ensure economic exchanges.   The rationality of the entrepreneur becomes defined by an adaptation to price
movements in the search for maximum profit.   It is within this
institutional universe that the industrial revolution based upon
merchant capitalism, mechanical techniques and free labour manifests
its full effectiveness in the accumulation of the wealth of nations;
it is achieved fully with the 'technical revolution' (Daumas, 1962)
in the middle of the nineteenth century and with economic liber-
alism.

The market mechanisms are spontaneous and the function of the
state is to maintain the rules of free competition.   The self-
regulation of the system is insured by fluctuations, which are the
necessary counterpart which it is neither possible nor desirable
to limit.   This autonomy of the market will be successively justified by the metaphysical belief in the natural order and by the
scientific law of the economic theory, whose most rigorous model is
the construction of general equilibrium;   the universal and supra-
historical validity fixes the scientific status of this theory at
the same time as it guarantees its ideological efficiency.

The blind belief in economic progress is alone capable of making
the acceptance of such a destructive economic rationality intelligible;   it proves inadequate in the most sombre periods dominated
by crises: economic thought expresses its pessimism in the nineteenth century with Ricardo's law of diminishing returns, Malthus's
law of population or, towards the 1930s, the theories of stagnation.

The market is an original historical creation; never before had
work and nature been considered exclusively as goods, never had
the economic been separated from the political, never had the individual been assigned the behaviour of homo-economicus.   It is
readily understandable that it may be claimed that a market economy
can exist only in a market society, as Polanyi (1957) does, but the
notion of the merchant society is a contradiction in terms because
by its very operation the market progressively destroys the equilibrium of the whole of society.

'Industrial capitalism' is established on a new technological
base and its growth is achieved by the internal concentration within
the branch of industry, by competition based on the differentiation
of products and by the distribution of the joint profit of that
branch between the holders of the oligopoly.   The formation of
stable monopoly and oligopoly situations and the broad economic
fluctuations bring about the intervention of the state.   At the
level of economic theory, these modes of organization and operation
are mainly expressed in the works of Chamberlin and Keynes.

The confidence in the efficiency of spontaneous market mechanisms
is weakened, and economic equilibrium results from a *construction*
by public and private authorities.   This economic form becomes
dominant from the 1950s, but the essence of the criticism is
acquired in the 1930s: Keynes demonstrated that the free play of
market forces does not necessarily achieve equality of saving and

investment;   Mayo observes that the industrial process destroys all
forms of social solidarity.   Both recommend deliberate intervention, in Keynes's case that of the state, in Mayo's view that of the
leaders of industry.

This constraint is essentially an anti-nature policy;   the basic
mechanism is no longer the market but public and private planning,
and this evolution is favoured by social awareness of economic development and by the partial control of the economic system which the
working class is able to exercise in a political democracy.

The intervention of the state, which initially is based upon the
growing awareness that the worker cannot be considered solely as a
factor of production and that his existence cannot depend totally
upon free competition on the labour market, is subsequently broadened to constitute a conception of the relationship between economy
and society.   Planning integrates two distinct requirements:
(a) rational organization of resources in order to achieve objectives deemed to be desirable, and (b) the promotion of ways of life
whose economic value is not directly measurable: 'Development is
not only towards affluence but even more, no doubt, towards the
construction of a society.   It has ethical implications which we
cannot evade: the values which we intend to respect and the ends
which we desire to pursue' (Massé, 1965, p.79).

This development presupposes changes in occupational structures,
economic concentration, urbanization, etc., but there is *continuity*
and *forecastability*.   Provided that one wants to do so, it is possible to create mechanisms for adapting to change, and to obtain a
'harmonized growth'.   The welfare state reconciles economic rationality and social rationality in so far as it ensures social arbitration and maintains the growth rate which has become a matter of
social consensus and the measure of ambition and economic success.

This extremely schematic presentation of the forms of capitalism
does, however, bring out the main dimensions of the comparison:
(i) the nature of the knowledge of production and the relationship
between its potentialities and the demands of the economic system;
(ii) the modes of relationship between the economic partners,
whether this is a matter of competition between firms or the equa-
tion of production and consumption; (iii) the level of development
of each of the economic forms; (iv) the manifest and concealed relationships between the economic institution and the action of social
forces.

One does not find a simple historical succession of these forms
of the economy;   rather *all three co-exist in the present actual
economy*.   There results from this, for the purposes of sociological
analysis, two tasks: (i) to distinguish facts according to whether
they belong to one or the other of these wholes and to determine the
way in which such wholes evolve;   (ii) to study for the various concrete units - enterprise, national economy, international economy -
the relationships of domination-subordination, opposition-comple-
mentarity, etc., between the three economic forms, it being understood that the influence of technological capitalism is not exclusively economic but also social and ideological. (1)

To examine this question, I intend to combine two modes of analysis which in the history of ideas have been falsely opposed, that
which concerns social practice and that which concerns the institu-

tion.   By virtue of the sociological tradition of which it is part, the latter concept has conserved particularly useful meanings: indeed, the institution is a whole and, thus, it leads to questions about the relationships between the parts.   An institutional analysis is relatively autonomous, and consequently any a priori of a mechanical and simple determinism disappears.   The relationships between institutions become a central problem and the institution manifests itself by different 'states' such that the comparative study of institutional modalities becomes a major interest;   there is also attached to this notion a set of philosophical, moral or political connotations which is merely contingent. (2)

This paper is therefore exclusively concerned with 'technological capitalism' considered as a new form of the 'economic institution'. It is as a function of the relationship between science and industry that we wish to determine the rules of its organization and operation and the conditions in which it is reproduced and transformed. It will then be possible to define the limits of an analysis confining itself exclusively to economic relationships, and to fix the 'sites' and the forms of influence of general social relationships.

THE FOUNDATIONS OF TECHNOLOGICAL CAPITALISM

It is by industry that man as a generic being exercises his domination over nature and constructs his objective world.   But to isolate from the general movement of creation of material goods and the satisfaction of collective needs the moment of production itself would be to refuse any understanding of the process of accumulation of economic wealth.   This process undergoes and manifests two extrinsic determinations, that of scientific imagination which serves as a potential for material power, and that of social relationships which in accordance with the rationality particular to the economic whole determine the conditions and limits of use of scientific invention.   The complexity of the real is sufficient to justify initially confining oneself to the historicity of the 'economic institution' such as it is determined by the 'knowledge of production'.

The scientific institution

Science has no origin;   it is co-extensive with a humanity which by means of language and technical skill observes and transforms reality and through myth and religion introduces into the universe an order which man experiences in his relationships with nature and his fellow men.

While the 'philosophical' revolution of the seventeenth century does not mark any absolute beginning, it does inaugurate a conception of nature different from those which preceded it and introduces a science which is new in its object and its methods.   As the heir of the Renaissance, this modern science produces a paradoxical history, since it is to destroy the dream of that period which gave rise to it: the construction of the unity of human culture and the mastery of universal knowledge.   Indeed, by virtue of its success, that is by its very act of foundation, it distinguishes itself from philosophy, from religion, from art and from technology, (3) and at the same time progressively forms a core of specialists, and a public, which are subject to a common system of specific social norms.   The scientific institution is born with its own purpose and ends, its rules of organization and functioning, its modes of recruitment and training, its system of sanctions and rewards;   it then becomes possible to study the modes by which it operates.

One might doubt what the issue of such an undertaking might be when one observes contemporary science, with its innumerable specializations and the complexity of their interrelationships.   While not being unaware of the size of the obstacles, it does, however, appear possible to determine with some rigour the principal forms of scientific institution from the particular point of view of the formation and evolution of 'knowledge of production'.   There are two terms here which are fundamental: (a) the typical relationships between the individual and nature, and (b) the organizational forms of scientific research.

The science of discovery and the science of transformation

The knowledge of production, which includes the set of scientific and technological knowledge used in the production of material life, can be apprehended from the point of view of evolution and the relative position of science.   This mode of analysis leads one to oppose the 'science of discovery' and the 'science of transformation' as two forms of the scientific institution.

The principle of this division is based neither upon 'states' of the theory nor upon sectors of science, but upon the dualism of conceptions of nature which are fundamental to present scientific practices.   Such a point of view should not only enable us to overcome meaningfully the diversity of fields of research;   in addition, in so far as interpretations based simply upon rearrangements of the field of knowledge, or upon analogies between intellectual structures and economic regimes, are open to criticism, it should enable us to define the process of a theory of knowledge which, by providing itself with adequate concepts, ensures that concrete mediations are not forgotten, those mediations by virtue of which an intelligible relationship can be established between two series of autonomous and specific phenomena.

While in an historic chronology the 'science of transformation' succeeds the 'science of discovery', it does not replace it.   These two institutional modalities therefore remain pertinent in order to characterize present forms of knowledge of production, but, for different historical periods, the division between scientific disciplines varies, and transfers are always possible from the former to the latter.   The evolution of sciences represents a privileged area which enables us to define the meaning of this analytical instrument. (4)

The science of discovery   The philosophy of the seventeenth century interrupted discourse on the origin of the cosmos and brought about

a crucial distinction between natural order and divine order;   even
when God is not absent from this world, he incarnates reason: the
secularization of the universe is not perhaps complete, but the real
is, however, rational.   A world which is at the same time secret
and 'logical' is the precondition of any research into the relationships between phenomena.   Being absent from nature, the scientist
gives himself the task of unveiling its laws:

> the term 'description' of nature began also to lose more and more
> of its initial significance as a living and striking represen-
> tation of nature;   it came more and more to mean a mathematical
> description of nature, namely the most precise and the most con-
> densed, but also the most complete collection of information
> under the relationships of law existing within nature (Heisen-
> berg, 1962, p.14).

It is this particular relationship of *an independent and free being
confronted by an enigmatic but ordered world* which defines the
'science of discovery'.

The scientific revolution of the seventeenth century changes the
relationships between the forms of the mind, substitutes modern
mathematical and experimental rationalism for the archaic rationalism of Aristotleanism, wipes out the qualitative physics of the
Middle Ages and of the Renaissance and replaces it by quantitative
physics.   It transforms divinity into a hypothesis which is simply
necessary to put the universe in motion and ceases to seek the metaphysical counterpart of its theoretical successes.   It becomes
intelligible, however, only when it is located in the transformation
of the distribution of resources and powers of traditional cultural
institutions.

The continuity of medieval thought was insured by universities,
by the church and by various forms of patronage.   The 'philosophers'
who devoted themselves to the observation of the facts of nature or
to speculative reflection could only do so as members of religious
orders or as teachers, as doctors and alchemists, dependent upon
princes and kings.   The 'new philosophy' encountered in these
powers devoted to the reproduction of tradition an opposition which
was so total and so rigid that it could only achieve its existence
by creating its own modes of communication, of recruitment, of
training, by ensuring for itself new sources of wealth, and by
instituting its own authorities and its own modes of legitimization.

As soon as it had resolved the main problems of its own autonomy,
science detached itself from the original institution;   the clearest
expression of this rupture is found in the refusal to pursue discussion with philosophers and theologians who are henceforth outside this new universe.   Subsequent development then modified the
internal organization and the relative position of the 'science of
discovery' within society, the basic essentials being established:
it exists in itself and as a function of a representation of nature
which has become perpetuated in numerous fields of present-day
science. (5)

From this period onward, the science of discovery manifests as
one of its major characteristics which is basic from the point of
view with which we are concerned, its difficult and ambiguous
relationship with the material ends of society.   In the eighteenth
and nineteenth centuries, science and technology designate two

series of different activities, two distinct mental universes, two
types of men, each a stranger to the other.   The technician,
'artist', 'engineer', 'enlightened amateur', devotes his inventive
capacity to applied mechanics and to methods capable of regulating
the forces of nature: he is the main subject of the industrial
revolution and of the extension of industrial mechanicism.   On the
other hand, the scientist, whose activity is orientated by the norm
of 'disinterestedness', devotes himself to the demonstration of
natural legality.   This break between science and production derives not only from the institutionalized values of an historical
period;   on the contrary, the opposition between the professional
codes of the scientist and the engineer only finds its true explanation because of the impossibility of justifying the practices of
the science of discovery by means of economic or technical utility.

The result of this is that in the nineteenth and in the twentieth
centuries, for certain branches of production *knowledge of production is dualistic*.   Procedures and products are modified in accordance with two distinct processes: on the one hand, the creation
of an autonomous mechanism for practical utilization of theoretical
knowledge (research and development), and on the other hand, technical pragmatism based on experience and ingenuity.   Science
occupies a distant position with regard to industry and the interaction between them can only be established by mediations which are
either unknown, or so complex and subject to chance that they fall
beyond the bounds of the risks which the economy can accept.

Research then designates autonomous intellectual operations and
the professional terminology - scientists, research engineers,
technicians, etc. - conceals differences of nature in the qualification of labour.   This relationship of exteriority makes it
impossible to mix operations and men belonging to distinct institutions.

The science of transformation   It is in the middle of the nineteenth
century that a new typical relationship clearly appears between man
and nature: scientific knowledge is no longer only assimilated to
the discovery of the hidden relationship between given phenomena,
it is also the promotion of a natural order.   For rational and
quantitative chemistry, the demonstration of natural legality depends upon the operation of *transformation of matter*, such that, and
this remains the essential truth of the science of transformation,
chemistry today has become the science of bodies which do not exist.
Industrial synthesis expresses in the most faithful form the formation of relationships which do not exist in 'given' nature, thus
attempting to construct unknown bodies, bringing into effect a
'factitious materialism'.   Henceforth, the scientist can no longer
maintain the illusion of the quest for the ultimate secret.   The
separation of the artificial and the natural loses all significance.
The experiment accomplishes at one and the same time two functions:
that of verifying laws and that of materializing knowledge.   Because
it is a deliberate creation, the history of nature is also a social
history.

The science of transformation determines the formation of an
institutional modality whose main terms can be grasped from the

nineteenth century onwards in which science is at the very foundation of industry.   Its products and processes are merely the
transposition of the scientific experiment on to the scale of economic production.   Research may be more easily conceived of as a
utilitarian activity which is deliberate and changing.   The social
composition and the rules of judgment of the institution directly
express this insertion of science: thus, research laboratories are
found just as much in industry as in universities;   the criteria of
knowledge are confused with financial criteria, and the bodies which
legitimize this activity can just as readily be scientific as economic, and the sources of finance are both public and private.

   The knowledge of production becomes unitarian.   Applied research
used as a pragmatic method of trial and error becomes very much
secondary, which removes all interest from the opposition between
science and technology.   The distinction between fundamental
research and R & D (Research and Development) does not introduce
any discontinuity into the intellectual process, because the division of labour and its concrete forms in terms of professional
qualifications and statuses changes in significance so that the
intellectual unity of scientists, engineers, and technicians is
re-established.

Analytical distinction and scientific disciplines   The two modalities of the scientific institution cannot be assimilated to two
scientific disciplines.   While it is true that in an initial historical phase, analysis enabled a comparison to be made between
physics of the eighteenth and nineteenth centuries and the theoretical beginnings of rational chemistry, the history of science
becomes subsequently so complex with its internal diversification,
the multiplicity of the interactions and the formation of 'hinge
sciences', that the qualification of each of these subdivisions
becomes a research problem.

   The greater part of industry still remains dominated by the
dualistic knowledge of production (science of discovery plus technology).   This is so whether one observes conventional energy
sources, metallurgy, or the motor car.   The science of transformation is found primarily in the chemical, pharmaceutical and electronics industries.   It is also valid for industry using, for
example, solid state physics, and it is exercised within new fields
such as medicine or biology.

   The history of science is simultaneously that of the reorgani-
zation of the totality of the cultural field, and that of changes
particular to this order of knowledge.   The two institutional forms
represent an initial instrument of analysis constructed in order to
discover similarities and differences (from a certain point of
view).   They serve to make structures and rules intelligible even
though they appear differently according to the disciplines and
historical periods.   They operate as a practical and theoretical
mediation between culture and socio-economic structures which allows
one to describe and explain socio-political organization which is
ordered in accordance with the demands of scientific knowledge.

Organizational forms of scientific research

This paper does not intend to present the evolution of scientific
research, an intention which in other respects would remain quite
obscure, but serves to introduce new dimensions of the scientific
institution.   Poor and private science finds in the state a new
source of financing as its contribution to national military and
economic power becomes greater, and receives an increasing part of
the national wealth.
   This intention reveals in part the classical interpretation of
the similarities between the sciences: intellectual co-operation,
professional communities and rhythm of development.   From the
second half of the seventeenth century in Western Europe and in the
USA, the academies and scientific journals exercise functions of
communication and legitimization, scientists acquire a high social
position and more and more of them receive a stable remuneration.
This growth of small science to large science, which has been taking
place for the last two centuries and a half, following an exponen-
tial curve, brings about a fundamental modification of the situation
of science within culture and society;   social thinkers very soon
came to consider this change as a decisive turning-point in human
history.   This unity does, however, come up against limits depending on the forms of organization and the rules of functioning of
scientific research.

Liberal science and organized science   The organization of research
varies according to the methods and levels of reference.   The
activity of reason after the desacralization of nature is hence-
forward applied to scientific work itself in order to reduce the
naturalism of 'genius' or of 'inspiration'.   This evolution, which
even affects the individual himself, is, however, very diversified
according to the 'types' and situations of science.   One can obtain
a synthetic view of the forms of rationalization of scientific
activity by distinguishing the main forms of intervention: (i)
fixing the quantity of scientific research (overall sum of credits);
(ii) fixing the relative importance of the various scientific disciplines (reasoned distribution of credits);   (iii) organizational
efficiency (deliberate concentration and organization of research
units);   (iv) programming of the objectives of research;   (v) administration of research;   (vi) technical division of scientific
work.
   At the present time the spheres of intervention of the state, of
major enterprises and of research centres, do not coincide and,
indirectly or directly, the large firm acts at every level of a
research policy.
   One may observe that the authorities who take decisions concerning research policies are rarely conscious of the a priori conditions upon which these decisions rest, that these postulates are
far from being quite evident, and that a discussion of them would
reveal philosophies of science that cannot escape objective criticism and whose utility would be all the greater in that research
activity within the enterprise is very often defined not by objectives but by the introduction of administrative procedures.   Thus

the forecastability of invention by programming and administration
of research is justified only by a conception of the progress of
science proceeding by accumulation and generalization which excludes
the theoretical discontinuity as a principle of change of scientific
knowledge.   As for the technical division of labour, it delegates
to organizational methods the capacity of fixing research strategies
and thereby presupposes that the moments and the terms of these
decisions may be the object of a sufficiently precise forecast to
enable them to be ensured by bureaucratic rules.   All this takes
place as if technical rationalization could apply indifferently to
the various human activities and, in the present case, without any
foregoing reflection on the *particular nature of scientific work*.

Autonomous science and heteronomous science While any scientific
discovery potentially possessed an economic or financial value, the
process of objectivization may be lengthy, indirect and somewhat
unforeseen.   The will - and the possibility - of orientating
scientific activity towards precise social needs brings about a
major institutional variation with the antithesis of science
orientated towards knowledge (autonomous science) and science
orientated towards the market (heteronomous science).
   Such a distinction taking account of the ends and purposes of
research activities differs somewhat from the usual classifications
which lend themselves more effectively to the demands of technical
rationality or of economic calculation;   it is characterized by a
high level of generality and its use in a concrete analysis implies
establishing a relationship with the terms of fundamental research,
research and development and applied research.   It is true that
this trilogy has already assumed the most diverse significances,
which may justify taking further liberties, and we shall therefore
define fundamental research as the whole set of operations of conceptual construction and formulation of general laws, research and
development as the series of activities using scientific knowledge
for practical ends, and applied research as the range of work based
on technical knowledge and whose purpose is to create processes
and products.   It seems logical to assimilate the first type of
research to autonomous science, and the two others to heteronomous
science.   But just as it is difficult to use these very specific
categories to observe a reality as ambiguous as that of scientific
work, in the same way the coincidence between these two sets of
terms is not absolute.   Thus the success of a R & D project may
depend on the progress of scientific theory and, consequently, on
the introduction of fundamental research orientated towards practical applications;   conversely, the solution of a theoretical
basic problem may demand specific means resulting from a R & D
activity whose end would be pure knowledge.   These cases are somewhat exceptional, but they do make it possible to specify that the
difference between autonomy and heteronomy is found also in the
decision-criteria of the researcher, be he individual or collective,
in the signification of what he considers as 'interesting'.   Thus
concrete strategies of scientific knowledge introduce - although
the persons involved are not necessarily conscious of this - two
conceptions of utility and thereby, the values of two types of
social authority. (6)

The initial distinction between the science of discovery and the science of transformation, combined with the two other dimensions, leads logically to at least eight institutional forms, but the true number upon which one may reason is more limited by virtue of the approximate coincidence between the two pairs which define the forms of organization of research.   One may therefore retain four modalities of the scientific institution: liberal science of discovery (autonomous), organized science of discovery (heteronomous), liberal science of transformation (autonomous), and organized science of transformation (heteronomous).   The analytical distinctions are, however, useful, for applied research on research and development orientated towards the market may nevertheless be carried out without programming or rigorous administration, and it is not impossible to conceive a gradual rationalization of a science completely devoted to fundamental theory.

What interests us here is less a systematic comparison of the various modalities of the scientific institution than *the bringing to light of organized science of transformation* and a study of the consequences of its use upon the process of production and exchange of economic goods.

A new economic form

The 'technologically advanced' enterprises or science-based industry are recent and imprecise neologisms used to designate a reality which goes beyond the bounds of traditional language.   But this descriptive localization does not determine the specificity and the limits of the phenomena under consideration, in which, in any case, it is not obvious that they may be determined without a necessary examination of the system in which they act.   However, one must not proceed by simple oppositions: that of the unit and the whole, that of micro-economy and macro-economy.   What in fact characterizes the 'technologically advanced' large enterprise is its potential capacity for omnipresent intervention and extension of the field of strategic interdependence.   This requires understanding and interpreting the conditions of its action in the organization and the functioning of the economic whole.   It is the particular combination of the organized science of transformation and industry which, in the abstract, enables us to characterize the new economic system with particular regard to the process of production and the function of products, and also the mode of competition which results from this.

Process of production and modes of creation of products

As it is usually used, the notion of technology designates very diverse realities: industrial mechanicism, automation or methods of production resulting from the application of science.   Here, I understand by the term technology *the whole set of phenomena which are part of industrial enterprise and which are directly the product of science, and more precisely of the organized science of transformation.*

The technological world is not given once and for all, it varies according to industrial branches and different historical periods and is continually being modified and enlarged.   For 'technologically advanced' large enterprises, it includes principally, at the present time, the mechanism and the administration of production, and the modes of creation of products.   Because it is analytical, such a definition has no obvious counterpart in concrete reality; it leads necessarily to a new delimitation of categories of phenomena, the similarity of the processes of influence and evolution becoming the justification for this unusual distribution.

The 'technical and scientific revolution' is inspired by a Utopia in which manual labour is unnecessary.   This prophesies the end of occupational alienation thanks to automated production (e.g. Richta, 1969), which amounts to an easy way of getting rid of the problem of power.   In contrast to this, the concrete study of science-based industry indicates, on the one hand, that the means of production cannot be considered from the point of view of technical rationality alone, and, on the other hand, that the phenomenon which most directly characterizes the economic system is found not in processes but in *products*.

As regards the ·administration of production, the use of mathematical tools and computers henceforth makes it possible to carry out operations which by their complexity have previously escaped all programming.   An extreme example is that of the space programme which has so remarkably kept up with manufacturing schedules, despite that numerous materials and processes which were ultimately involved in it were unknown at the time of the initial decision. Their production required the integration of a high number of different activities which were very risky.   An analysis based upon the systematic examination of alternative choices and on ordonnancement (7) methods enables us to elaborate policies for new products whose specifications one is able to determine without yet knowing the means of achieving them, and at the same time to manage rationally a large number of diversified goods.   It reduces the part of intuition, of 'recipes', of 'precedents'; it renews the relationship between social integration and the technical process of production, and finally, by virtue of its specific characteristics, it radically modifies the conditions for the extension of industrial mechanicism.

Indeed, the rapid substitution of mass products brings out the tension of *forecastability* and of *flexibility* as a vital problem for the production machine.   From this point of view, automation should be considered as one form among others of the forecastability of production - neither the most forecastable nor the least costly - the rigidity of which becomes a definite handicap for active strategy.   All forecasts with regard to the rapid and inevitable extension of automation have shown themselves to be false.   An interpretation of its history would be better understood in an analysis of the movement of goods and of the system of relationships between industrial groups.

The new fact from which all the appropriate conclusions must be drawn depends upon *the rapid renewal of products created by research operations integrated within the production system;* the organized science of transformation becomes the basis of industrial strategy.

The result of this is changes in the nature of the product, in the
rhythm of its renewal and in the relationship between production and
consumption.   Products crystallize more technical capital and more
knowledge of production.   This intensive and extensive artificial-
ity, which increases continually and which involves an increasing
number of products, modifies not only the composition of capital,
the duration of investments, etc., but also the symbolic significance of the goods.

For about ten years now the progression of the relative importance of the creation of products as opposed to that of production
processes has taken place in spite of occupational, organizational
and social tensions.   These have in part been limited by the extension of production management.   This primacy of new products over
the improvement of production processes has brought about a streng-
thening of competition corresponding to a new rule of the game and
a new phase of the economy.

Technological (oligopolistic) competition

If, in an oligopoly situation defined by the strategic interdependence of groups, by the joint profit of the industry and by competition by production costs and products, differentiation is inherent in economic competition, it is none the less true that by
changing its rhythm this economic competition changes its form, and
that the notion of 'monopolistic competition' (Chamberlin, 1953) (8)
conceals the particular characteristics of the relationship of
domination between major enterprises and between production and
consumption.

To use the term 'technical (oligopolistic) competition' is to
take account of the fragility of the partial monopolies actively
established by industrial groups.   This development results from
two distinct sorts of facts: (i) the stable control of clientele
presupposes a passive consumer who, by virtue of ignorance or as a
matter of routine, becomes and remains a member of a particular
area of the market.   Now the democratization of education increases
the number of purchasers capable of establishing comparisons and of
changing from one market to another, and the 'politicization' of
consumption accelerates this fragility;   this results in a potential
mobility of consumers which diminishes the probability of stable
partial monopolies.   (ii) when new products take advantage not only
of experience or know-how, but also of the organized knowledge of
production, and in particular the science of transformation, the
universe of potential competitors increases considerably and compels
industrial groups to modify their market position rapidly.   The
field of real and potential competition becomes so vast that it
makes it impossible to enter into implicit or explicit agreements
at the level of the branch of industry and requires of the oligo-
polists, in order to survive or to achieve victory, to adapt to an
accelerated rhythm, of technological innovation.   This is the
'universalism' of economic antagonisms which makes the establishment
of relatively stable partial monopolies a more precarious process,
if not in fact preventing it completely.   To confine oneself to the
term of oligopoly alone would be inadequate, for this is simply a

formal statement; the behaviour of firms in fact obeys the operating rule of the economic system of which they are a part - in this
case technological capitalism.

The combination of a new clientele and a particular intervention
of human intelligence in the process of creation of new goods therefore radically modifies the forms of competition between the groups
within industry.

Technological capitalism

The high level of economic concentration is the primary and pre-
dominant reality of modern production, and Galbraith draws an infer-
ence from this observation when he defines and studies the 'industrial system'.   It will be readily admitted that the relative
dimensions of assets or technical capital represents a significant
characteristic in that it conditions the choices and the reference
periods of the enterprise, but the 'size of the enterprise' dimension is ambiguous and there are disadvantages in placing in one and
the same category a variety of sectors ranging from telephones and
telecommunications to trade, and including transport or mines.   It
will, moreover, be noted that Galbraith's analysis enables us to
explain the differences between company policies of those firms
which are part of the 'industrial system' and those which are outside it, but cannot take account of the internal diversity within
the 'industrial system'.

If, as a supplementary criterion, one chooses the notion of technological innovation, it cuts across the 'industrial system' and
enables us to regroup in a single class the science-based industries
(financial, technical and intellectual concentrations governed by
the new form of competition), more particularly at the present time,
chemistry, pharmacy and electronics.

To avoid any confusion between reality and an analytical schema,
it must be explained that *there is no single branch of industry nor
any economic unit which pertains wholly to technological capitalism.*
This limitation is explained by the diversity of the activities and
of the markets of multi-national groups and also by the novelty of
this economic form.   The heterogeneity of the real leads us to make
distinctions between phenomena according to whether they derive from
one or the other mode of the economic institution and to study the
various combinations between the actual relationships.   Only the
'leading' major enterprises are dominated by the rationale of technological capitalism; these are the so-called *large technological
enterprises.*

To summarize, technological innovation reinforces economic concentration, raises the level of production and intensifies competition through products, since such competition can only be regulated
with great difficulty at the level of the branch of industry by
virtue of the extension of potential competition based upon the
relative universality of the science of transformation.   Technological (oligopolistic) capitalism is defined by *the articulation
of science-based industry and of a new form of competition in its
rhythm and its forms.*

THE FUNCTIONING OF TECHNOLOGICAL CAPITALISM

Empirical economic categories are useful for public or private planning but they are not the best means of discovering the invisible
and structured reality which enables us to explain at one and the
same time the functioning of the economic system and the represen-
tations made of it by those participating in the social scene.

Analysis enables us to identify 'technological capitalism' by a
particular combination of science, of industry and of competition;
it is therefore in its functioning that this economic form shows its
full originality in that it is governed by the principle of power
(puissance) and, so, it 'betrays' traditional economic categories
and reasonings.

Power (La puissance)

The fact that political economy tells us so little about contemporary reality is because it is basically dependent upon a certain
conception of knowledge.   One can claim that the discovery of universal and eternal laws represents the only authentic scientific
project but in opposition to this one could agree with Marx when
speaking of the classical economists: 'Thus there *was* history, but
there is no longer any history.'   But if one admits the change in
the nature of economic activity as indicated by the particularism of
the large technological enterprise, the new forms of competition of
the ambiguity of consumption, if one conceives of observable economic reality as the product of the combination of three pure forms,
then scientific interest shifts towards the discovery of the laws
specific to each of these units and the process of bringing to
light the rules of transformation.   In a period of rapid and radical evolution, the abstract universalism of economic science readily
appears to be the discourse of those addicted to the past, and in
any case shows itself to be incapable of formulating a legitimate
basis for objective knowledge since it is unable to determine the
limits of its validity.

Technological capitalism, as a whole based upon interdependencies
between the large technological enterprises and upon codified social
relationships, functions in accordance with a concealed principle,
that of *power (puissance)*.

This term does not cast any light upon the nature of the participants but designates the mode of action of a collectivity which
is itself considered as a system of social relationships.   In comparison, in merchant capitalism, the general equilibrium was derived
from the activity of individual enterprises faced with the market
situation and devoted to the maximization of profit.   In industrial
capitalism, first of all practice and thereafter, theory, had demonstrated that the collective interest could not be deduced merely
from the interplay of individual interests, and that the subordination of industry to social ends could only result from the intervention of the state.   Consequently the dynamics of the system
depends upon a complex interaction of economic activities and policies.   Very schematically, one could maintain that the source of
each of the forms of the economic institution is profit, growth and
puissance.

Puissance is an ambiguous concept since it designates at one and
the same time both the capacity to do something, i.e. to produce,
and the capacity to impose one's will upon others.   Its originality
lies in the complex relationships between these two meanings.   As
capacity to produce, technological capitalism reveals its singular-
ity in the social valorization and the industrial achievement of the
indefinite reproduction of goods and services.   The basis of the
economic system, as indeed of the large technological enterprises
which go to make it up, lies less in the satisfying of collective
needs than in the use of all the potential of the rational combination of science and industry to enable the human race to bring about
a material transformation on such a scale that it modifies the
balance of nature in major respects.

The will to power is found not only in national and international
economic relationships but also in socio-political relationships;
however, the struggle between large technological enterprises cannot
be reduced merely to the intention of winning positions within the
international industrial hierarchy, maximizing profitability or
accumulating capital.   It appears also by means of predetermining
the choices of others, as a deliberate imposition of a particular
conception of the economic order.

Indeed, it is the necessary relationship between these two forms
of puissance which defines technological capitalism.   The production of material life for whatever purpose, which means that it is
its own end, becomes the only accepted principle of competition and
this economic struggle may appear in all the more extreme forms in
that the capacity to impose a certain universe of merchandise
appears as a legitimate project.   The concrete mode of being of
competition is basically determined by the historical conditions of
the combinations of the forms of capital and social forces.   Towards
the second half of the nineteenth century the generalized use of
technical inventions and of commercial capital and the domination of
an industrial and commercial middle class which won over the state
in order to impose upon it the mode of action which was compatible
with economic development, gave rise to competition and, therefore,
led to a concentration which reached a state of balance in the 1920s
and 1930s.   Similarly, the coming together of a certain amount of
knowledge of production with financial capital, meeting in association with the universalism of the economic field, brings about a
weakening of the intervention capacity of social forces, since it is
exercised through the medium of a state which has lost a major part
of its means of action and leads to a renewal of the trade war and
of industrial concentration.   The decline of the process of economic regulation by the market and by the state explains the blind
character of the economic process, and favours the impact of puissance as an extremely vigorous motive which, having become its own
end, perpetuates the present form of the economic system.

Puissance is not directly observable and in this respect appears
to differ from profit or growth.   In fact, this difference is only
apparent and to demonstrate this one needs only mention, in the case
of profit, the multiplicity of profitability ratios and the uncertainty of their meanings, and, in the case of growth, the equivocal
nature of the notion of rates whose value depends upon development
phases, which involve adding together 'utilities' and 'disutilities'

and which tell us nothing about the quality of the mode of life.
This difficulty of method is indeed genuine, for as a capacity,
puissance can only be measured indirectly in terms of its effects,
which are often incommensurable, or by an evaluation of its resources
(financial capital, technical capital, capital of knowledge, etc.),
and this cannot be a mere listing but must also include the modes of
use of these resources, i.e. will and competence.   In any case, it
is not vital to enter into a methodological discussion here, for the
main terms are well known, thanks to studies on local communities,
even though fully satisfactory solutions have not yet been found.

The fundamental question concerns the relativism of the empirical
forms of the relationships of power.   According to the historical
period, the states of the economic system or the social and political environment, the competition will be exercised through short-
term profitability, the rhythm of technical innovation, the reduction of human labour, prices, etc., and depending upon its position
in the industrial hierarchy, each large technical enterprise must
conform more or less closely to the criterion adopted by the dominant enterprise;   it is then easier to understand the diversity of
ratios or pragmatic formulae which one finds in economic literature
about the industrial enterprise.   Puissance as a domination of
social existence and as the social relationship of domination may
appear in the concrete form of a decision criterion which operates
along the full length of the chain of ends and means.   The various
criteria represent not only a form of rationality, i.e. a coherence
in the commitment of resources, but also a certain conception of
the 'correct' mode of economic action.   As a mode of intervention
by the economic institution and as the principle of the relationship
between enterprises, these criteria represent modes of rationality
which I shall refer to as *logics of action;*   they are in competition, and to discover the objective conditions determining the hierarchy of logics of action such that one can observe them in the
actual practices of enterprises and industry becomes an essential
research problem.

The homogeneity or heterogeneity of the dominant logics of action
enables us to qualify the interrelationships between large technological enterprises and it is clear that these are the product of
economic forces and social forces, and not merely of the modes of
management of the organization.   That technological capitalism is
so often experienced and thought of as an autonomous system deploy-
ing itself freely as a function purely of the rule of puissance is
no more than an illusion resulting from initial observation.   In
truth, the theory of technological capitalism must necessarily be
based upon the relationships between economic domination and social
and political domination.   Puissance is not an 'instinct', it is
the mode of economic relationships resulting from the combination
of a form of production of material life with a form of social relationships.

To admit puissance as the operating principle of an institutional
modality is also, and necessarily so, to assign oneself the task of
reconstructing the economic field in so far as it brings together
all the elements which directly - by their production - or indirectly - by their capacity to modify the volume and the distribution
of resources and to transform the situations of the activity of the

enterprise - weigh upon the concrete modality of the creation of
wealth and upon the predetermination of the decisions of actual or
potential competitors.   In the case of large technological enterprises, it will be understood that this field is international and
that, from a particular point of view, it includes the influence of
the state and of social forces, not to mention the more complex
phenomenon of the division of the world according to levels of development.

With regard to the present period and as a general rule, the precondition of the implementation of puissance is the profit rate, the
means of action residing in the tension between possible technological discontinuities and probable markets, with results being indicated by the growth of capital.   The consequences of this represent
a permanent transformation of social existence.   To be more precise, each enterprise which, through the form of its capital, has a
certain economic ubiquity, must use all the knowledge it possesses
in order to create a specific market before others do so.   Its
occupation of this market will necessarily be transitory.   This
results in differentiation and diversification of which there are
two main causes: (i) the same body of knowledge of production can
be used in various ways, which leads to the development of different
departments in industrial groups, an opportunity which, if not
taken, represents an economic loss; (ii) in the art of war, one
must protect oneself against risk by increasing the probability of
success or diminishing that of failure by multiplying the opportunities for battle.   The increase of goods and services of the enterprise therefore depends also on the systematic use of all 'idle
capital' - financial, intellectual, and technical - and a rational
management based upon the coherence of decisions and programmes.

Technological capitalism lives by its capacity to transform
inventions into economic goods, to make the most recent products
created by the use of science into desirable products and to eliminate the value of previous goods.   Now the paradox of this form
of economy derives from the fact that its *purpose is largely unde-
termined,* since this faculty of industrial creation and production
may be applied with equal facility to armaments, the building of
new towns, the conquest of space, the manufacture of medical products, etc.   While it may be admitted, on the one hand, that the
influence of synergy, i.e. the continuity routed in the past,
becomes progressively less and, on the other hand, that technological innovation is not the product of an historical necessity, the
basic question relates to the choice made by the economic system to
produce certain goods and services and not others.   How can one
explain the composition of the universe of the merchandise of technological capitalism?

Such an interrogation does not call into question economic rationality, for this notion is just as pertinent in evaluating the
efficiency of the use of means as it is foreign to the analysis of
needs which one has chosen to satisfy, this analysis being a matter
of politics.   The paradox of a technological capitalism which seems
to evolve in accordance with its own system of dynamics, which produces goods and services which in consequence modify human nature,
is that it cannot base this process on reason; there does, of
course, exist a dynamics of technological innovation, but the direc-

tions it takes can be very varied, the solvability of demand seems
to justify supply but the distribution of income is not exclusively
an economic fact, and, above all, the satisfaction of demand can be
achieved by very different means.   The composition of the universe
of the merchandise, which implicitly expresses a model of society,
cannot be explained at the level of the economy alone but also depends on social structure in so far as this, by distribution, by the
mechanisms of reproduction of national and international hierarchies
(revenue, prestige, etc.), by the forms of the division of labour
and by general social relationships, determines the possible spaces
of economic activity.

The subversion of economic categories and reasonings

The value of the interpretation of the economic system in accordance
with the principle of puissance depends upon its capacity to explain
the data collected.   It is, however, possible to test its validity
indirectly by examining certain forms of economic reasoning with
regard to the relationships between industrial capital and banking
capital, to the fixing of prices and to the function of profit.

Capital

The myth of the top 200 families or of the powers of finance dies
hard, and recent crises in certain industrial and commercial companies resolved by bank loans can only strengthen the imagery of
an economy governed by occult and all-powerful forces.   It is
therefore all the more important immediately to formulate as a
general proposition that the multi-national large technological
enterprise, unless there are exceptional circumstances, enjoys considerable autonomy with regard to the power of the banks.
    In order to establish the terms of the discussion, one must now
introduce three distinctions, the first of which relates to the
places in which capital is formed: *industrial capital* results from
the activity of the enterprise, and *banking capital* is held or created by the banks and by the state.   The second distinction refers
to the forms of capital: *technical capital* comprises the processes
and products (equipment, stocks, etc.) necessary for the production
of the goods and services, and *money capital* designates the liquidities of the enterprise.   The third distinction relates to the
modes of use of capital: *financial capital* includes the mechanisms
of management designed to obtain a profit based upon money capital,
and *productive capital* the effective use of technical capital in
order to act upon the market.
    Technological capitalism is characterized by the domination of
industrial capital, which is exercised according to a variable
relationship between productive capital and financial capital.   This
definition does not coincide with that of imperialism such as it has
been formulated by Lenin, since the possible predominance of financial capitalism does not imply any necessary supremacy on the part
of the investor or the financial oligarchy over the industrialist.
The superiority of the large technological enterprise resides in

the volume of money capital which it can control through self-
financing mechanisms and direct access to the money market, in the
lack of power of small shareholders and the passivity of institutional shareholders.   The autonomy of the directors of the large
technological enterprise results from the arbitration which they
may exercise as between technical capital and money capital, from
the disproportion which exists between the needs of industrial
groups and the supply of banking capital, and, finally, from the use
of money capital for purposes which are no longer exclusively industrial.   The function of management of liquidities exercised by the
banks is not, however, eliminated but is often part of the overall
strategy of the large technological enterprises. (9)

In technological capitalism - which is international and competitive - the enterprise, in order to conserve its autonomy or improve
its position in the industrial hierarchy, must satisfy two contradictory requirements: the mass production of diversified goods and
the capacity to intervene in markets in order to attack competitors
or respond to them; the form and the modes of use of capital represent decisive economic choices.

Indeed, the increase of the volume of fixed capital which characterizes the modern economy represents a severe constraint, for it
necessarily creates a rigidity which limits the possibilities of
strategic change, and thereby places the large enterprise in a fra-
gile situation.   This vulnerability can be attenuated by organizing
technical capital or by rigorous private planning.   It must, however, be admitted that the administration of production encounters
limits in the necessities of mass production and that the medium-
and long-term determination of the objectives and means becomes a
very chancy business.   On this last point, and although Galbraith
states that the large enterprise controls its environment and can
therefore develop private planning, direct observation indicates
that the large technological enterprise operates within a situation
marked by a high degree of uncertainty which results mainly from
the composition of the world of competition, from the overall evolution of science and technology and from their effects on methods and
products, from industrial relations, politico-economic phenomena,
etc.   This uncertainty is experienced in concrete terms in the present phenomenon of private 'deplanning' in favour of strategic
action combined with forecasting.

If one excludes from the analysis those purely speculative forms
of enterprise which are conglomerates, whose heterogeneity results
merely from seeking maximum short-term financial profitability (even
though the pathology of a social system may also enable us to grasp
the objective truth of the situation), the large technological
enterprise defined by coherence together with industrial diversification and continuity, ascribes all the more importance to money
capital as opposed to productive capital, in that the markets represent high risks in which the conglomerates are also active.

Ten or fifteen years ago, self-financing was considered as a
simple practice enabling the large firm to choose an industrial
policy independently of the variations of the financial market; it
was the means of ensuring the autonomy of industrial directors over
bank directors, of separating the two 'worlds' of industry and of
finance which seem to obey different rules, sometimes indeed oppo-

sing rules.   It was a way of achieving the ability to reason in
the long term rather than the short term.   The significance of this
break has changed today following the very high level of capital
demand of the large technological enterprises, which is all the more
difficult to satisfy where the economic unit does not occupy the
leading positions in the international industrial hierarchy.   Whatever may be the sources of money capital, the large technological
enterprise must necessarily take account, on the one hand, of the
comparison between rates of financial profitability, and, on the
other hand, of production levels which maintain its industrial identity, and, by the acceptance of risks connected with new products,
ensure its participation in the system of creation of collective
riches.   That which was separated is henceforth brought together
within the context of industrial capitalism, and this development
finds its organizational expression in the increasing influence of
financial departments.

The new form of the economic institution thus modifies the relationships between industry and banking.   Unless the banking organization itself undertakes both functions, i.e. industrial and financial, financial departments which, along with the introduction of
industrial strategy, enjoy great autonomy in conducting their own
policy, appear best adapted to the requirements of the technological
economy; the capacity simultaneously to exercise control over movements of investment and movements of capital indeed represents one
of the necessary conditions belonging to the international economy,
in so far as it represents an optimum choice in order to obtain
high profits and maintain the flexibility of the production mechanism compatible with industrial choices and risks.

Technological innovation transforms and thereby renews the forms
of capital (and of the labour force); this development operates in
the direction of *immateriality* and *mobility*: capital, like knowledge of production, no longer has a stable material expression;
both can be used for the most diverse ends.   This results in new
rules for the functioning of the economic institution.

Price mechanism

Technological capitalism is characterized by the *arbitrary fixing
of prices*, i.e. by the importance of determinations other than
impersonal market forces.   The economic theory of relationships
between competition situations and price levels is rigorous, and
indicates that in large-unit capitalism dominated by monopolistic
competition the process of bargaining includes the elasticity of
demand, the relative influence of firms and the consciousness and
experience of competitors' reactions.   Prices may consequently vary
between the minimum fixed by production cost and the maximum represented by the overall revenue of the industry.   In fact the stability of prices in the short and medium term is a practical reality
which is explained by collusions with a view to maximizing joint
profit of the branch of industry concerned, whereas over a long
period the gradual decrease of the price of goods enables new markets to be created.

A situation of technological oligopolistic competition upsets the conditions in which the discretionary power of the corporation is exercised and implies a new economic reasoning.   The autonomy of the large technological enterprise is reinforced by the control over clientele, although the situations are partial and transitory, by the domination of the enterprise over the consumer.   This domination is based upon the controlled obsolescence of products which makes it impossible to establish a relationship of equivalence between prices and the quantities of utility satisfied as a consequence of the rapid renewal of the bases of comparison and by organizational complexity, which enables true decision mechanisms and criteria to be concealed and rules out any verification of the validity of the price levels fixed.   Conversely, the discretionary power of the enterprise is weakened by the impossibility of reasoning right across the industry concerned in order to determine the maximum joint profit, and by real and potential competition which compels the enterprise not only to act upon different markets (products and nations) but also to maintain this deterrent power which appears in the form of the renewed diversification of products.   According to situations and circumstances price levels may vary but the general process remains the same, continuous revision of public or semi-public contracts being merely the equivalent of the activism manifested by the major technological enterprise in the private market.

While this form of competition does not impinge primarily on prices, it is, however, possible to observe considerable variations, in some cases downward variations, which depend basically upon the composition and structure of the clientele.   From this point of view, large technological enterprises do not represent a homogeneous category, and one must distinguish at one extreme the aerospace industry, which lives almost exclusively on state orders, and at the other extreme, the chemical or electronics industries in which more than half the turnover comes from private customers.   The fragility created by any monopolistic situation is further aggravated when the purchaser is the state and may suddenly revise its objectives by political decisions which take little account of questions of industrial continuity and the conditions for the survival of enterprises;   in this latter case, strategies then appeal to pressure groups and obviously are not part of the classic schema of supply and demand.

The arbitrary element in the fixing of prices does not necessarily indicate the existence of excessive profits but expresses the potential strategy of large technological enterprises, which they may in fact introduce to a greater or lesser extent as a function of their oligopoly position and which is based on a *specific relationship between the products sold and their profitability phases*.   The existence of the field of discretionary power resides in the capacity of the large technological enterprise to maintain or to enlarge the range of products which is in that phase of their life, thus giving the greatest degree of liberty to the power of the enterprise. (10)   Such a policy in its extreme form presents specific difficulties.   Examples of these are the coincidence between input and output of ranges of goods, the relationships between new production costs and the amortization of old equipment, the consequences of error on the new market, etc.   While in principle such a policy raises the rate of profitability, this proposition must be considered as a *tendency* which at the present time cannot be empirically verified;   indeed there is no measuring instrument in existence enabling us to compare the profitability of a classical industrial policy with that of a policy based upon the rotation of products.   Moreover, the introduction of such a strategy is so complex that it readily leads, especially when the financial, organizational and other conditions have not been evaluated, to deficits which can bring about the disappearance of the enterprise as an autonomous power centre.   These failures should not, however, be permitted to conceal the efficiency of this form of competition, which in large measure explains the high level of industrial concentration that has come about in the last decade or so in the USA and in Europe.

The true limits of discretionary power of the large technological enterprise reside in the maintenance of national and international economic equilibria, which give rise to complex problems of analysis such as that of the co-existence between investment movements in multi-national groups and international financial relations, and of the respect of the conditions for uninterrupted growth which presupposes a minimum level of coherence of interventions by the state.

But in a world system which combines the three forms of the economic institution in accordance with the most diverse relationships, these constraints remain very little understood.

The function of profit

Any economic system deriving from industrial civilization creates profit.   Thus having made this general observation, one has not said very much;   in fact the true problems lie beyond this point.

Neither the diversity of sources of profit nor the conditions by which we define that which belongs to technological capitalism enables us to identify the function of profit;   one must therefore examine its significance in direct terms as regards both large technological enterprises and the whole of the economic situation.

The large technological enterprise does not necessarily give priority to the search for profit and it may attribute or find itself compelled to attribute greater importance to the rhythm of technological innovation, the increase of turnover or the increase of the volume of assets.   Moreover, profit rates may vary considerably from one period to another.   It is always possible to affirm that the underlying rule in this diversity is the maximization of profit in the long term, but it remains to be seen whether this is merely a metaphor or a precise reality;   this leads us to switch levels and examine the economic system.

The concept of maximization of profit may carry two meanings, one relative and the other absolute.   In the first case, maximum profit is assimilated to the firm which obtains the best results and this is the pragmatic approach which was adopted by the new generation of economists when they considered that the enterprise seeks the maximization of turnover under the constraint of profit (Baumol, 1959), the maximization of the rate of growth compatible with security (Marris, 1961), or that it obeys a utility function including the direct or indirect remuneration of the directors of the enterprise (Williamson, 1963).   While one or the other of these formulae may account for the fixing of the mass or the rate of profit, it in no way enables us to demonstrate that the level chosen by the leading firm is the highest possible.   This being so, one returns to the second meaning of this concept, i.e. the mode of determining the maximum theoretical profit.   This question has a precise meaning in 'merchant capitalism', when the enterprise is sufficiently flexible to seek equality of marginal cost and marginal receipts, but changes its meaning in 'industrial capitalism', when the enterprise is defined primarily in terms of a branch of industry and the revenue of this branch may be known;   it becomes possible to determine the rate of maximum profit with the major reservation that in a dynamic economy the distribution of the national wealth between the various industries is subject to a continuing process of bargaining.   On the contrary, when the basis of action is an indeterminate number of branches, as is the case for the large technological enterprise, this calculation can no longer be made and the concept of maximization of profit loses all precise meaning: the result of this is that the conditions for a demonstration are no longer present.

To this logical consideration must be added another which concerns the economic system in so far as it is subject to the contradiction between competition and profit;   for real and potential competition as an expression of the organized science of transformation and of the diversified and omniscient strategy brings about a rapid obsolescence of a technical capital which cannot be entirely amortized, and, more generally, the rhythm of increase of fixed capital may become higher than that of profit margins, which leads to a decrease of the rate of profit for the group of enterprises as a whole having a relationship of strategic interdependence;   in the extreme case, a whole industry becomes the victim of this competition mechanism, and finds itself in overall terms in deficit and can no longer ensure its continuity except with the help of the state.   This pathological form in which costs are dissociated from profits indicates the existence of a dynamics specific to the movement of renewal of products which falls outside the bounds of the rule of profit and which may prevail in case of opposition.   This primacy of competition is explained by the absence of balancing mechanisms which derives from the paucity of experience of interactions between competitors and from the narrow limits of intervention of the dominant firm or of the state.

Thus profit represents the condition or the result of the activity of the large technological enterprise, a mechanism for allocating economic resources and distributing revenue, and is certainly not the operating principle of technological capitalism.   It is possible and indeed probable that this form of unbridled competition is only transitory and that a new equilibrium will be restored at a higher degree of industrial concentration, but in this case one would then have to study a new form of the economic institution.

CONCLUSION

Technological capitalism is both the mode of production of economic
goods and the organization of scientific creation; both its functioning and its transformation depend upon the necessary combination
of, on the one hand, the scientific process which is achieved by
means of economic innovation and which contributes its own vitality
and, on the other hand, industrial activity which ensures favourable
conditions for the deliberate construction of the real situation.
In its unhindered movement, this economic form, which in this respect is similar to the first phase of industrialization, is objective evolution and existential change; it is experienced in production and consumption as liberation and servitude, as creation of
works and autonomy of things.

   Because it is specific, this development should not be too
rapidly assimilated to known forms or functions: it also represents
the first halting steps of an emergent institutional modality which
claims to achieve definition by its products.   In addition, this
assimilation should be cautious because the understanding of its
internal mechanisms remains fragmentary.

   To overcome this difficulty, is to establish an intelligible
relationship between the essence of the process and its concrete
expressions, between the operating principle and material manifestations whose terms are antinomic.   The large technological enterprise acts in accordance with provisional and contingent compromises
in a situation where the terms of one alternative can at no time
eliminate the other, for such a result would be merely a form of
exclusion from the economic system or the sign of change in the
institutional modality.   The real meaning of technological capitalism can only be discovered by the knowledge of the tensions which
are inherent within it, as, for example, those which exist between
forecastability and technological innovation, planning and strategy,
mass production and renewal of products, market control and diversification.

   The principle of puissance, in so far as it combines a set of
specific resources and a form of struggle, profoundly modifies the
position and the sphere of economic relationships.   Analytical
instruments, such as supply, demand, utility, propensity, etc.,
are valid only for institutionalized economic systems.   It is a
marginal line of thought, running from Marx through Schumpeter and
to Perroux, which has taken an interest in a theory of the history
of economic systems and has brought to light the role of force,
and of violence in the development of industry.   Now the new form
of economy, more than all those which have preceded it, must be
studied from the point of view of domination: domination of technological capitalism over industrial capitalism and merchant capitalism, domination of the richer nations over the poorer, domination
of the more independent large technological enterprises over those
which are less so.

   The combination of these forms of domination explains the influence of American society, for it is quite clear that the formation
of multi-national groups in no way eliminates national reality, and
those French or European large technological enterprises which count
upon public power to limit the degree to which they are subjected

to such constraints are well aware of this.   The name of this
international domination is *imperialism*, which in general terms may
be defined, as Schumpeter put it, as 'a quest for power as an end in
itself';   it is inherent in technological capitalism, the mainspring
of which is puissance, and it transforms inequality into power relationships since freedom of choice becomes more and more restricted
as one moves further from the peak of industrial success.

This relationship proves to be particularly important in that it
predetermines the needs which the dominated large technological
enterprises intend to satisfy.   As an economic mechanism, it produces global effects which influence both culture and politics,
since it imposes upon societies whose historical traditions are both
diverse and original a delimitation of the sphere of the merchandise
specific to the USA.   Thus imperialism designates more specifically
the operation - whether deliberate or unvoluntary, conscious or
unconscious - by which a model of society becomes, in the name of
economic rationality, the common reference of those countries which
derive from the same exchange system.   While competition reinforces
domination and favours social and cultural integration, which
further limits possible choices, technological capitalism - because
it is international and competitive - can only increase the importance of domination relationships.   Henceforth, the dilemma becomes
clear: to adopt the ends and means of the most powerful industrial
groups in order to fight them on their own terms is also to accept
their value system, whereas to maintain one's originality is to
destroy the unity of international exchange.   Cultural exporting is
all the more effective and insidious in that it claims to be exclusively economic, and imposes a system of objects which is not
neutral, since it is the vehicle of the meanings, the cleavages and
the conflicts of the society which gave birth to it.

By virtue of its capacity for incessant material creation and the
strength of the determinations which it represents, technological
capitalism necessarily introduces the question of the links between
the economic base and general social relationships, with the problem
of the state assuming a high priority.   While in an economy based
on the branch of industry and the nation, the state has been able
to acquire real influence and to guarantee access to power by pop-
ular social forces without this being considered as illusion or
dupery, the situation changes when public intervention is limited
out of respect for the rules of private international competition
and is therefore subject to the demands of technological capitalism.
Very schematically, the state assumes three distinct functions:
direct or indirect aid to the major technological enterprise, particularly when the latter is threatened with exclusion from the
economic system, regulation of the national economy, and management
of the results of growth, whether these are favourable or unfavour-
able.   These facts are well known.   If we do not pursue our analysis of the relationships between economy and politics further,
this is not because the question is a minor one but because it presupposes a sociological theory of the state which at the present
time does not appear to have gone very far.   It must simply be
noted that the primacy of technological capitalism as such necessarily produces a weakening of the state, which is all the more
marked as the disunity increases between its field of intervention

and that of the large technological enterprise, which may freely
carry out international transfers of intellectual, technical, and
monetary capital; thus one can explain its dependence with regard
to large technological enterprises, which also means the decline
of control of the economic movement by social forces.

The autonomy of the economic system does not give rise to major
difficulties with regard to the institutional agents - this can be
understood by referring, where industrialists are concerned, to
Saint-Simon's doctrine of progress and, as regards scientists, to a
belief in the international community of science - and the more it
appears as a specific reality governed by a particular logic, the
more it seems necessary to produce a quantitative description of
the parts of which it is composed.

The disappointing results obtained from such a practice are the
best demonstration of the 'economistic' illusion on which it is
based.   Indeed, certain realities are not capable of any economic
explanation, for example the delimitation of the field of merchandise; and in other cases, for instance the division of social and
technical labour, the end purposes of economic development, the
rhythms of growth or consumption, historical experience has proved
that they could be modified by means of social and political struggle.   This observation enables us to formulate the two essential
questions concerning the functioning of technological capitalism,
namely the contradiction between the extension of the political
field and the reduction of capacities for social intervention, and
the tension between the conditions of belonging to this economic
system and conflicts within national enterprises.

Fewer and fewer phenomena are now considered inviolable or
natural, but the diversification of the values at stake in social
struggles is accompanied by a differentiation of the participants
in the social drama - collective workers, users, urban collectivities, etc. - and by a fragmentation in terms of categories, which
is the product of abrupt development and of frontier barriers pro-
tecting national particularisms.   The maintenance of the conditions
of this tension between 'politicization' and the powerlessness of
collective action is also a perpetuation of technological capitalism.

Within the various countries concerned, one can see the formation
of this 'new policy' which draws together objectives, means and
hitherto unknown participants in an action aimed at controlling
the economic process.   Even when it is explicitly defined purely
in terms of claims, this intervention on the part of social forces
is also a management activity by virtue of the counter model, both
cultural and social, which it carries within it, and in terms of
the constraint which it exercises upon the resources of the large
technological enterprises situated in secondary positions, and
therefore directly threatened in terms of their survival.

The economic process thus conforms all the more strictly to its
function of the generation of goods in accordance with the principle of puissance as the discrepancy increases between its field
of action which is often quasi worldwide and that of the political
system which is in general national.   By the fact alone that they
act upon an international scale, large technological enterprises
necessarily limit the intervention capacities of social forces -

whether groups or countries - and present problems which are insol-
uble from the point of view of the social forces, since any action
upon one part or element cannot affect the whole, but may bring
about the disappearance of the element concerned. This situation,
which is also a collective experience is at least liable to call
into question so-called 'economic' activities which are difficult
to separate from the other areas of social life, from theory, and
from political thought on the nation, the state and justice; its
consequences are, however, highly ambiguous, for it may just as well
favour historical blindness and the provincialism of social practices as it may ensure the birth of a reflection about the 'good'
economic society, uniting in their relative autonomy the levels of
the enterprise, of the nation, and of the international community
as a whole. Whether autonomous or dependent, technological capitalism only yields up its secrets if one studies the forms of the
division of labour, stratification, social classes, the state - in
short, the bourgeois society.

NOTES

To avoid any misunderstanding I should first like to establish that
this analysis is no part of the various theories of post-industrial,
post-capitalist or post-historical society. Its aim is more limited. In no way do I believe in the formation of a society different from the preceding one. Although it is necessary to study the
relations between the economic system and the political system,
cultural fashions, class relationships, etc., for brevity's sake it
seemed more useful to me to go more deeply into the examination of
the relations between the economic system and the scientific system.
To the extent that the economic system frees itself from national
political powers and appears as a 'natural' phenomenon, which
imposes itself upon everyone, without any need for discussion, its
reproduction is also an invisible and indirect reproduction of class
relations. The enterprise is considered as an empirical reality
which allows one to identify the rules of organization and the functioning of the more general system of which it is a part.
  1 'In all forms of society, it is the specific conditions of a
     particular production which assign to all others their rank and
     their importance. This is a general clarification, in which
     all colours and shades are present and which gives to these
     their singularity. It is a particular ether which determines
     the specific weight of everything salient which exists within
     it' (Marx, 1965, p.261).
  2 We should here specify that the institution is a construction
     of the observer from an observation of a confused concrete
     reality, that consensus is always precarious, threatened by
     relationships of exchange and power, and finally that its func-
     tioning depends on internal competition between institutional
     values and ends.
  3 One must distinguish the institutional reality from the practice
     of scientists, for this break is applicable to the former but
     not to the latter. The 'philosophers' of the seventeenth and
     eighteenth centuries continue the rehabilitation of manual work

and ensure the conjunction of craft activity and the theoretical
tradition; they are interested in and directly participate in
the construction of the mechanisms necessary for experience,
while their conception of a mechanistic world gives rise to a
basic reflection on the relationships between the functioning
of machines and the 'machine of the universe'. But professional specialization brings about the disappearance of the
Renaissance man who is at one and the same time artist, scientist, and engineer, and the interest of scientists in technology
will lead only to the formation of an industry of scientific
instruments; mining and industrial exploitation is not influenced by the progress of science. This unintentional autonomy
becomes all the more apparent in that science and industry are
to develop more rapidly and in accordance with the necessity
which is specific to each.

4 For the history of science and technology see in particular
Bernal (1957), Daumas (1957), especially the remarkable chapter
by Lenoble on The Origins of Modern Scientific Thought (pp.367-
534), and for the theory of knowledge, Kuhn (1962).

5 While contemporary physics has abandoned the idea of nature 'in
itself', since the knowledge of phenomena is not independent of
the position of the observer or the experimental instrument,
there does however remain a fundamental difference between a
nature which changes its meaning according to the questions
which the scientist asks and a nature created or transformed
by practical experimental or industrial activity.

6 The margin of choice available to researchers in their professional activity is underestimated (and scientific ethics is
often very convenient from this point of view), as is also the
(unconscious) influence of social values of institutions and
social groups. But here one would have to carry out more
detailed research into the history of research and the various
moments marked by decisions whose rationality is limited if any
by the impossibility for the individual to evaluate all consequences of alternative choices. The reconstitution of these
decision processes combined with the study of the effects of
the international scientific community would enable us to
explain the more privileged or more neglected directions of
research.

7 This term has no precise English equivalent, but may be taken
to mean the whole process of controlling manufacturing from
beginning to end (Eds).

8 Perroux (1953) indicates the full importance of the Chamber-
linian revolution in the introduction to the French version of
this book. For a general judgment, see Bain (1967), pp.147-76.

9 The study of the power within the enterprise must be considered
as an essay using the available literature and limited empirical
observation. The problem is confused because too often two
distinct questions are confused: the distribution of shares
and the fixing of economic policy. Thus the owners of the
means of production (the heads of the enterprise, financial
groups, shareholders) who are thought of as concerned with maximum short-term profits are seen as in opposition to the directors who are more interested in the maximization of long-term

profit. However, it is *logistically* unnecessary to introduce
this distinction between the groups in terms of motivations in
order to account for differences in the policies of the enterprise, and it should be sufficient to take account of the principle of functioning of the economic system; moreover, this
thesis has not been empirically verified.   In fact, for all
large technological enterprises financial profitability appears
as the *condition* of the introduction of the industrial strategy
independently of the 'objective interests' attributed in a more
or less arbitrary fashion by the observer to the various groups
which go to make up the political system of the enterprise.
One may have doubts about the relative importance of the directors and the financiers in the large technological enterprise -
my own feeling is that the former represent the dominant group -
but whichever answer one gives, it does not have any particular
consequence upon economic choices.

10   For reasons of simplicity, the product is considered as the unit
of technological competition.   In fact, such an analysis is
too general, for the first element is the product/market with,
therefore, for a given product, phases of life which are variable according to the markets; management, forecasting and
strategy thereby become more complex.

Chapter 5

ORGANIZATION AND PROTECTION

Arthur McCullough and
Michael Shannon

INTRODUCTION

The analytical framework of modern organizational theory views
organizations and the state as separable, rational, self-conscious
and self-determining entities: they can interact voluntarily, without protection and without loss. This paper begins by formulating
the main assumptions of organizational analysis.

Against the dissociated view of the state and its limited definition, the paper emphasizes its protective functions that developed
historically in relation to organizations, and argues that all
organizational transactions have been conditioned by state protective power which always remains present in one form or another.

Protective power in relation to organizations is clearly revealed
when it fails to operate legitimately, for example in Northern Ireland. In such cases the functions and roles of many organizations
tend to change in ways that cannot be explained by organizational
theories. It is suggested that so far as historical analysis of
the protective power of states can be advanced, the possibilities
of the disintegration and emergence of organizations will crucially
relate to the character of withdrawal or intrusion of protective
administrative, military, or legal apparatuses.

The study of organization today does not usually imply very much
about nationalism, colonialism, imperialism, absolutism, feudalism,
capitalism, revolution, war, indeed any large-scale changes of civilization in the modern - not to speak of the ancient - world. Much
of contemporary social science, according to the introduction to a
recent book on capitalist agriculture in the sixteenth century,

> has become the study of groups and organizations, when it has
> not been social psychology in disguise. This work however,
> involves not the study of groups, but of social systems. When
> one studies a social system, the classical lines of division
> within social science are meaningless. Anthropology, economics,
> political science, sociology - and history - are divisions of
> the discipline anchored in a certain liberal conception of the
> state and its relation to functional and geographical sectors of
> the social order. They make a certain limited sense if the
> focus of one's study is organizations (Wallerstein, 1974, p.11).

Whether there is a liberal conception here or a tradition of some
kind, would be rather difficult to say, although it is fairly certain that one can probably grasp the bulk of organizational theorizing in terms of a loose outline of assumptions and presupposi-
tions that will be outlined below.

In the first place it would hardly be an exaggeration to say that
the themes related to modern organizations bear a striking resem-
blance to the vision that western political thinking had of individuals in the eighteenth century.   That is to say, organizations can
be roughly considered as contracting parties, effectively free to
enter or not to enter into any particular exchanges.   They will
not generally enter into any exchange unless they benefit from it
and co-operation can therefore be achieved without coercion.   The
organization is seen as almost morally complete at birth and not
depending upon submission to authority or dominance to provide its
identity, moral purpose or completion.   Rather, its existence
begins when 'explicit procedures are established to co-ordinate the
activities of a group in the interest of achieving specified objectives' (Blau, 1968). (1)   This is a voluntarist-instrumental view
that has been emphasized particularly strongly by recent writers on
organizational analysis.

One view has emerged, for instance, in which organizations are
seen as a tool needing techniques or technologies applied to some
kind of 'raw material' which is transformed into a marketable product (Perrow, 1970). (2)   In another case, what impels organizations to action is assumed to be a certain notion of rationality
for which the epistemological basis is that 'Instrumental action is
rooted on the one hand in desired outcomes, and on the other hand
in beliefs about cause/effect relationships' (Thompson, 1967,
p.29). (3)

In such terms organizations can be conceived as conceptually
distinct and removable analytically from the world around them, and
it is accordingly on such a foundation that an examination can proceed of organizations, and at the same time of the organized relationships that may vary from one body or type of body to another in
time or place.   Hence the proliferation of studies about schools,
churches, persons, prisons, hospitals, businesses, social welfare
agencies, military institutions and so on.   There is, of course, a
variety of attempts to examine the field in which such organizations
live and its interactive relationships with the organizations themselves, and there are even general attempts to dimensionalize environmental forces as more or less complex, turbulent or uncertain
(e.g., Emery and Trist, 1965).   After the initial extrication of
the organization has been completed, however, the business of its
reincorporation through environmental transactions is academically
fixed more or less within the initial scheme of assumptions. (4)

A further notion that may be imported heuristically in order to
describe the general tenets of modern approaches is that of beha-
viourism, at any rate in so far as that doctrine supposes that the
determining influences on action must always be fairly immediately
observable.   Thus the determination and consequences of organizational behaviour are necessarily embedded within an interactional
matrix which tends to resemble a communications chart.   Connections
are, in fact, often crystallized in information terms or in bio-

logical systems models, and where an interaction is not at least vaguely conceivable in this realm then it is quite often excluded altogether.   The power of an organization would therefore be established by observing the effectiveness of its actions, vis-à-vis its significance to others with whom it has various dealings, and any possible imbalance of power would have to result from such dealings.   Alternatively, of course, the existence of differences of power or resources can be made to rely on the rather more existential differences of initial endowments or conditions of scarcity. (5)   This is really the last resort, but legitimate enough as long as inferences are not made about present positions from, say, before the life of the organization has begun, or beyond the boundaries of its communication devices.   By now there is virtually no chance that the fate of a certain company might be connected with that of a certain peasantry or might be implicated in some foreign national revolt.   Industry may have definite linkages with the military but it could hardly have ties with a peasantry.

Perhaps it is worth adding that in one guise or another, there are pluralistic elements attached to the modern organization which are most likely to restrict it to incremental changes.   Thus,

Task environments of complex organizations turn out to be multifaceted or pluralistic, composed of several or many distinguishable others potentially relevant in establishing domain consensus (i.e. common expectations amongst interacting organizations). This appears to be true even of organizations embedded in totalitarian political economies, since for any specified organization there appears to be alternative sources of some inputs; the several kinds of inputs required come under the jurisdiction of different state agencies; and there are alternative forms of output or places for disposal of output (Thompson, 1967, p.29).

And from another exponent we may note that 'retaining or gaining power is difficult because it is almost always contested' (Perrow, 1970, p.15).   Or again, 'from the fact that there is a plurality of actors and of goals and a scarcity of instruments, it follows that social actors will tend to resist each other in the sense of hampering each other's actions' (Thompson, 1967, p.100).   In other words, there appears to be an implicit behaviouralist assumption that the direction of change ought to be observable as well if change is to be deemed to occur.   If a corporation would have all the capabilities to produce 100,000 motor cars tomorrow as well as today, this would not seem to involve much change from one day to the next!

Finally, it may be noted that in so far as a view of the state is implied by organization theorists, it is usually that the state is itself a characteristic organization that operates regulatively in the interstices of other organizations and is checked both internally by the aims of its members and externally by those of other organizations whose interests it ultimately safeguards.

From traffic control to development administration, it may be said with confidence, modern administrative and policy sciences and organization studies have provided a variety of models that have no wider - and certainly no deeper - foundation in social scientific reasoning than this schematic outline.   Perhaps there is an ideo-

logical function in a behavioural, functionalist, pluralist framework whereby it is exceedingly difficult to locate the relations of
exploiter to exploited except possibly within the confines of
market-democratic reasoning.   The integration of systems and scientific formulations in social organization at the same time indicates
the technical possibilities of social science as an instrumental
productive force in capitalist planning and legitimation.   There is
an impressive barrage of conceptual obstacles that precludes the
theoretical designation of organizations within a totality of political economic relationships.

If the study of organizations was conducted not as an articulation of market bargaining models but in relation to the total
social system through which they are constituted, then the locus of
authority and exchange relationships might conceivably be viewed
not in terms of pluralistic distribution but rather as a unified
technological domination.   Thus, Marcuse notes,

> Contemporary society tends to be totalitarian.   For totali-
> tarian is not only a terroristic political co-ordination of
> society, but also a non-terroristic economic-technical co-ordin-
> ation which operates through the manipulation of needs by vested
> interests.... Under the rule of a repressive whole, liberty can
> be made into a powerful instrument of domination (Marcuse, 1964,
> p.16).

Marcuse is here attempting to see western organizations not in
relation to market ideology but in terms of their total co-ordinated
or discordant transaction with the rest of the world.   Democratic
organization (and its associated intellectual framework) is seen as
predator in relation to other territories or even in certain spheres
of its own domain. (6)   In a sense, this possible shift of perspective is rather crucial for organization studies for on the one
view, as an example, the modern multi-national corporation can be
seen in opposition to various nation states and other corporations,
or on the other, business corporations and nation states would be
seen as dependent and interdependent in a repressive world division
of labour based on exploitation.   Nevertheless, the dominant framework of organization studies has taken the former perspective in
which the interests of the multi-national enterprises are seen
contradicting those of national communities represented by their
sovereign states.   That this issue should have arisen at all in
western social science is somewhat remarkable since a vast proportion of wealth that gave birth to the European state was produced
by multi-national type operations in areas such as East India and
the Belgian Congo.   For several hundred years political decisions
affecting them have been taken outside these countries, but only in.
recent times when the centre of capitalist power has shifted to
America and Japan, and many western nations begin to take on peri-
pheral characteristics themselves, does the question of nation state
versus multi-national enterprise really take shape.   Here then is
a way of putting one of the critical issues for modern theories of
organizations: they are both unhistorical and ethnocentric.

It is interesting that a model which not only predicates the dissociation of various public agencies but also the dissociation of
the organization of business, and of the nation state, should find
such general acceptance in the face of evidence which shows the
interpenetration of these interests in their historical development.

There is certainly a great deal of truth in the notion that the
state safeguards the interests of its constituent associations, but
there is no reason at all to assume that it does so most importantly
against their own competition rather than against an outside nation
or in some colonial endeavour.   The point is really that all of
the organizations compared and classified in different countries or
regions by organizational analysts in terms of their memberships or
prime beneficiaries, bases of compliance or structural characteristics, etc., (7) may be themselves organized in relation to a
nation state and to a global balance of power involving competing
nations.   Nations themselves may not even be the most significant
organizing feature of a modern world economy.   New alignments and
power blocs continuously emerge and it is these which globally
determine the total organization of organizations in such a way that
they may be structurally connected despite the lack of apparent
immediate contact required by organizational analysis.   The image
shifts, broadly speaking, from a sea on which ships collide or coa-
lesce without their shockwaves extending much beyond, to a planetary
constellation in which all movements are interrelated by gravita-
tional laws.   It makes a lot of difference which of these two
images is more or less historically relevant, and it can be argued
that the first one, appropriate to modern analysis, has been unrea-
listic since approximately the beginning of the sixteenth century.
(8)   In particular, the notion of the state as a somewhat larger
ship safeguarding and regulating the conduct of smaller vessels and
recently turned upon by growing combines of the latter, owes very
much more to modern interpretation than to any given historical
reality.

From the many years that organizational diagnosticians have spent
as consultants to both public and private agencies, it should be
painlessly obvious regardless of all the control systems, tarrifs,
safety devices, credit stipulations or legal regulations that
operate both through the economy in general and within a particular
organization, that although many survive and succeed, many more
dwindle or disappear, and of them most would probably have argued
that so-called protective regulations instituted by government with
respect to manpower or trading, or some other aspect of business,
were likely responsible.

Which organizations precisely, one might be inclined to ask, are
being guarded and against precisely what?   Surely the state can
never be cast as a *general* protector even within its own territory?
On the contrary, a relatively convincing case can be put forward
for the view that, at any rate, throughout the period of its formation, the state and in addition many corporate enterprises can be
more easily represented as racketeer than protector.   Difficulties
begin, notes an economic historian,

> when we consider the racketeer who collects payments for 'pro-
> tection' against a violence that he himself threatens, and who
> actually supplies a sort of 'black-market' protection in return,
> suppressing rival gangsters.   Such borderline cases are far
> from negligible when we consider the violence-using and violence-
> controlling enterprises of Europe during the millennium between
> AD 700 and 1700.   Which princes were rendering the service of
> police?   Which were the racketeers or even plunderers?   A plun-

derer could become in effect the chief of police as soon as he
regularized his 'take', adapted it to the capacity to pay, defended his preserve against other plunderers, and maintained his
territorial monopoly long enough for custom to make it legitimate
(Lane, 1966, pp. 414-5).(9)

On this basis it can be argued that the state comes into existence as a monopolizer of protection and that the fortunes derived
from this in early modern times may well have been a more important
source of profits than even superiority in industrial techniques or
industrial organization. For the enterprise engaged in international trade or colonization during the first centuries of Europe's
oceanic expansion there were, indeed, all kinds of payments to be
made:

These included convoy fees, tribute to the Barbary pirates, or
higher insurance for voyages into pirate-infested waters, bribes
or gifts to customs officials or higher authorities, and other
kinds of smuggling costs. It included some expenditures by
trading or colonizing enterprises to organize their own armed
forces - from placing extra guns and soldiers on an individual
ship to despatching an army for the defence or even the conquest
of a colony (ibid., p.374).

The extent to which transactions can be predictated upon the
mobilization and exclusion of social forces and loaded with civil
and political power is totally lost within a structure that both
assumes voluntariness and relegates constraint as a predisposing
factor in exchange. On the contrary, it may be argued that *all*
capitalist transactions have been conditioned by state protective
power which remains present always in one form or another. If an
organization has developed under protective auspices it might gain
enough force to struggle against the form of protection offered in
relation to whatever dues required where these are no longer advantageous. But in this case 'freedom of movement' will only mean
freedom from a particular source of protection and control whilst an
alternative form has been set up. Indeed, part of the notion of
freedom of trade, of laissez-faire, imagines that the state has
grown up autonomously and externally to material life, and can,
therefore, just as easily be excluded from interfering as it can
be invoked regulatively in economic affairs. Yet the image of the
state as protective conveys precisely the notion that mechanisms
of defence and security are necessarily employable. Thus for a
number of causes the monopolistic growth of protection occured in
early modern Europe.

In connection with the economic depression of the fourteenth and
fifteenth centuries, it has been argued that the phenomenon of
'gangsterism' of nobilities was extremely widespread throughout
Europe and manifested itself in outbreaks of lawlessness by noble
groups and attempts to conquer new territories. At the same time,
the dissolution of feudalism took various forms, but always involved
the expropriation of groups who had generally no greater recourse
than to criminal activity or impinging on the established trading
of others for an adequate livelihood. (10) In addition, brigandry
related to expansion of overseas trade was perhaps the most difficult to check, and especially amongst foreign competitors.

How then, should protection and order emerge from such dis-

array? (11)   Frederick Lane has put forward the suggestion that in
the use of violence and violence-controlling enterprise there will
under certain circumstances exist great advantages of scale when
competing with rival violence-using enterprises or establishing a
territorial monopoly:

> to be sure, there have been times when violence-using enterprises
> competed in demanding protection in almost the same territory,
> as for example during the Thirty Years War in Germany.   But such
> a situation was even more uneconomic than would be competition
> in the same territories between rival telephone systems.   Com-
> peting police forces were even more inefficient than competing
> fire companies (Lane, 1966, pp.390-1).

Hence in the building of absolute states at the end of the Middle
Ages, the princes could contrive monopoly profits by protection and
organized bureaucracies devoted to that aim (the principles of
organization and rationalization of such bureaucracies were later
to become incorporated in other large companies).

In medieval theory, the right to trade, under protection, was a
privilege to be bought mostly from the princes.   It then became an
exclusive property right, and the guild thus 'enfranchised' with
its 'liberty' could demand that the coercive power of the state be
turned against those who infringed its monopoly privileges.   A
historian of the English reformation recalls that in 1601 a member
of parliament asked, when a list of monopolies was read out, 'Is
not bread there?'

> His irony exaggerated only slightly.   It is difficult for us to
> picture to ourselves the life of a man living in a house built
> of monopoly bricks, with windows (if any) of monopoly glass;
> heated by monopoly coal (in Ireland monopoly timber), burning in
> a grate of monopoly iron.   His walls were lined with monopoly
> tapestries.   He slept on monopoly feathers, washed himself with
> monopoly soap, his clothes in monopoly starch.   His hat was of
> monopoly beaver, with a monopoly band.   Out of monopoly glasses
> he drank monopoly wines and monopoly spirits;   out of pewter mugs
> made from monopoly tin he drank monopoly beer made from monopoly
> hops, kept in monopoly barrels or monopoly bottles, sold in
> monopoly-licensed alehouses.   He shot with monopoly gunpowder
> made from monopoly saltpetre.   He travelled in monopoly sedan
> chairs or monopoly hackney coaches, drawn by horses fed on mono-
> poly hay.   He tipped with monopoly farthings (Hill, 1969, p.38).

Trading in monopolistic companies was agreeable to governments
in fact because they were easiest to control whilst trade was seen
primarily as a source of revenue.   The companies were also themselves, therefore, exploited and plundered by governments.   As the
Venetian ambassador summed up the situation in England in 1622,

> although favoured by various privileges, the companies are dec-
> lining owing to the charges laid upon them by sovereigns ... and
> because to maintain themselves they are compelled to disburse
> great sums to the favourites, the lords of the Council and other
> ministers.... Thus *burdened* and *protected* they are *enabled* and
> *compelled* to tyrannize over the sellers without and the buyers
> within the kingdom (cited in Hill, 1969, p.24).

It may have been agreed in general that sixteenth- and seven-
teenth-century trade should amass wealth, yet clearly 'increasing

the national wealth' begs a number of questions.   Wealth for whom?
For the business community?   For the state?   Did merchants exist
for the state or did the state exist to help the merchants? (Hill,
1969, p.76.)   There are superordinate factors here in addition
because these European states developed only in relation to each
other and to the expanded possibilities of competitive commercial
trading through overseas empires and divisions of labour with
eastern European countries. (12)   Hence it was within the context
of international rivalries that state monopoly protection became in
the latter part of the seventeenth century enshrined in national and
colonial policies.   Thus, for example, the Navigation Acts and the
laws associated with them that gave English ships a monopoly of imp-
erial trade by stating that ships trading to the plantations should
all be of British or colonial build involved, in effect, a reorgan-
ization of trade policy from one based on monopoly companies to one
based on national monopoly.

The largest chartered trading companies, such as the East India
Company, would argue in national terms when taking measures against
interlopers:

We are engaged, no doubt on business principles, on securing for
the English people a part of that trade which has been successively the monopoly of the Portuguese, the Spaniards, and the
Dutch.   No doubt the produce which we bring is dear.   But we
have reduced the price.   Had it not been for our efforts,
Englishmen would have to pay whatever price the Dutchmen might
choose to exact.   The expansion of our trade is, moreover, the
expansion of English enterprise.   We train seamen by the hun-
dreds; we have, it being necessary for our trade, an armed
marine which is part of the national forces, as it assuredly
would be used, did needs arise, for the national defence (see
Rogers, 1920, p.120).

It was also argued by Frederick List, a German political econo-
mist of the nineteenth century, that this kind of protective alli-
ance was able to operate - and, indeed, was enhanced - in and
through the principles of free trade that were professed in Britain
from the latter part of the eighteenth century.   Thus, for example,
in relation to India, free trade was not adopted till her relative
manufacturing power had been stamped out by protection against her
industries, and then free trade was forced on her so as to prevent a
revival (see Dutt, 1903, p.302).

'I demur, in especial,' said a colleague of List, 'to the free
traders' contention that when two nations exchange goods, both
derive equal benefit from the exchange.   The varying amount of
capitalized energy with which the respective nations work will
always produce a difference in the national benefit, for the one
endowed with more capitalized energy will have a natural advantage' (quoted by Spann, 1930, p.197).

This superiority of manufacturing power would not, however, stem
from the branches of industry alone, but rather in its total relationship to state property which, List noted,

'does not by any means consist exclusively of the returns from
the lands owned by the State, etc., or of the capitalized value
of such incomes.   All the defensive powers of human beings and
of the land; armies, fortresses, weapons, the administrative

art of the civilian state in its entirety; even the constitution,
the laws, and the national memories, are constituents of state
property' (ibid., p.200).
War, for instance, could be considered the creator of powerful and
vivifying energies within the state, and as part of its protective
strategies.

Hence the possibility of the state as an independent intervening
or regulating device occurs only within the restricted definition of
organizational theory.   Total government laissez-faire is a contradiction in terms because no modern government can *not* influence
economic life.   As E.J. Hobsbawm puts it,

Any government activity - any system of public laws and regulations - must affect economic life, quite apart from the fact
that the least interfering government rarely finds it possible
to abstain from controlling certain obviously economic matters
such as the currency.   What is at stake is not the fact of government intervention, or even (within limits) its weight, but
its character (Hobsbawm, 1969, p.226).

In the seventeenth century the state created monopolies in order
to sell them, and in addition to those connected with an industrial
process there were monopolies for licensing which gave permission
to break the law: the state actually traded in the sale of exemptions from its own legal restrictions.   The modern state is equally
capable of affecting industrial development in the opposite way by
offering relief from tax laws, normal requirements of planning permission, exemption from import or export duties, in addition to the
more 'positive' incentives of direct grants and subsidies.   Hence
governments will compete against each other by offering a wider or
more attractive range of exemptions to industrialists and, despite
the likelihood that modern industries implanted in this way may
seldom market their products or obtain the bulk of raw materials in
the 'host' country, the problems of unemployment and consequential
loss of political prestige may enhance the relationship.

Considerations of this nature raise the hegemonic as against the
liberal pluralistic or countervailing nature of governmental and
industrial organizations.   Thus when the advantages that normally
accrue to governments (in terms of political prestige or avoidance
of critical social demands) by maintaining or extending supportive
apparatuses to industrial organizations are no longer certain, or
reaped only at too high political costs, the ultimate withdrawal of
protection becomes imperative.   This can be seen, for example, in
decolonizing situations where an alternative regime to direct rule
may provide a more legitimate basis for specialization and trade in
the colonized country without economic loss to the colonizer.   The
costs of extending full protection to citizens abroad may have
become too high in relation both to the advantages sustained by
industry and the possible damage to legitimacy where supportive policies necessarily require too drastic or 'undemocratic' actions.

As a particular example, this situation has become increasingly
apparent in Northern Ireland where the possible forfeiture to industry was made clear from the Ulster Workers' Council immobilization
of production by cutting off a major source of electrical power.
Political apparatuses can no longer be extended indefinitely in this
context and several companies estimate the consequences through con-

tingency plans for withdrawal of personnel from the province and at the same time redirecting corporate strategic plans.

When the state can no longer offer protection to citizens and trades as is evidently the case here, the inadequacy of modern organizational analysis is at the same time clearly revealed.   In 1969 Catholic districts of Belfast and Derry established 'no-go' areas where the authority of police or army could not apply or was severely limited - a strategy that was soon copied in Protestant communities since in these circumstances people turn to the most powerful institutions in their neighbourhood (unless intimidated to leave):   these may be the church or chapel, ad hoc community assoc- iations, and usually the dominant forces of para-military organi- zations (the combination of religion and armed men controlling loca- lities is reminiscent of feudal relationships).   In return for 'loyalty' they offer protection either from themselves and opposite numbers, or from a hostile community with an authority underlined by murder, knee-capping, beatings-up, and masked presence on the streets.   As a recent study of political assassination in Northern Ireland states:

> in the vacuum created by the absence of the Royal Ulster Consta-
> bulary, the effective control of law and order in Protestant
> working class areas passed to the para-military bodies.   Here
> again there is a parallel with Catholic areas.   The hard men
> on both sides of the sectarian divide are usually punctilious
> in their enforcement of the law when it comes to non-political
> offences.... In the absence of traditional law enforcement the
> para-military bodies have taken over (Dillon and Lehahe, 1973,
> p.277). (13)

Other spheres of influence also emerge and pass to different organi- zations: social centres and lucrative drinking clubs;   welfare and community associations;   newspapers, and even self-help industries; whilst local entrepreneurs, shopkeepers and publicans may find part of their profits extracted for protection.

When in 1974 the government failed to remove barricades from the roads and failed to stop intimidation and could not, or would not, enforce the will of the Executive, the daily running of Northern Ireland passed into the hands of the Ulster Workers' Council strikers (see Fisk, 1975).   Within a few days the protective pat- tern of everyday life was radically altered.   Farmers, industrial workers, service industries, individuals on social benefits, mana- gers, even civil servants, all became increasingly dependent on the patronage of strikers who allocated petrol and issued passes allow- ing selected personnel to work and supplies to be moved. (14) Organizations and individuals had to adapt to what appeared the most powerful protective institutions, and the more the people did this, whether from conviction or fear or simply to get their basic nece- ssities, the more the strikers gained legitimacy.   Eventually the elected local government could not function and resigned its pro- tective status to parliament.

The classifications of organizations into religious, welfare, voluntary, custodial, etc., with their associated means of com- pliance or bases of legitimacy ranging from coercive or remunerative to moral, are in effect entirely disrupted by this pattern of events and the relevant memberships or beneficiaries of many organizations

may have altered beyond all recognition.   Moreover the relationships between organizations are no longer identifiable because their
character has totally changed, and to crown everything, the singu-
lar mediating body - government - that ought to be pluralistically
entwined with all these developments, no longer exists.   It can
hardly then be an intervener or even an instrument of certain corporate or community interests as conceived in the versions of social
organization reviewed above.

The difficulty is largely that having conceptualized *all* organizations including the state as positive entities, there is basically
no way of ascribing failure to such processes of violence, intimidation, obliteration and war which are themselves constituted by
organizations in interaction rather than by the various hostile
workings of an abstract environment.   It becomes reasonable then
to seek for alternative formulations of social interaction that will
attempt to incorporate the organization of exchange across more
diverse or multiple modalities, an attempt that will at least seek
to determine the totality of relationships rather than merely inter-
pret exchanges in a particular way.   As an economic anthropologist
has argued in relation to the concepts of primitive exchange,

It has to be understood that trade between primitive communities or tribes is a most delicate, potentially a most explosive,
undertaking.   Anthropological accounts document the risks of
trading ventures in foreign territory, the uneasiness and sus-
piciousness, the facility of a translation from trading goods to
trading blows.   'There is a link,' as Lévi-Strauss writes, 'a
continuity between hostile relations and the provision of reciprocal prestations.   Exchanges are peacefully resolved wars,
and wars are the result of unsuccessful transactions.'   If primitive society succeeds by the gift and by the clan in reducing
the state of war to an internal truce, it is only to displace
outward, onto the relations between clans and tribes, the full
burden of such a state   (Sahlins, 1974, p.302).

From this kind of exchange conception it is possible to acknowledge significant disruptions between organizations that may have
previously appeared to interact mutually and harmoniously.   Modern
organizational theory must remain silent precisely because its formulation of exchange is inadequate: at each stage of analysis emerging forces are characterized as new-born entities with exactly the
same organizational features as those no longer visibly in existence.   The problem of order, accordingly, is relegated to some
peculiar inverted version of a Hobbesian state of nature. (15)

Paul Baran noted in the context of economic growth that in their
dealings with advanced nations the euphemistically dubbed 'undeve-
loped' nations have been continually hampered and restricted in
achieving their potentialities - the whole field should be dealt
with in terms of *obstacles* to development from their point of view
(Baran, 1973).   The relative positions of organizations or nations
as more or less 'developed' can hardly be ascribed to general tendencies of growth or decay or to any inherently propelled dynamic,
but as A.G. Frank (1967, p.9) argues, 'development and underdevelopment are opposite sides of the same coin.   Both are the necessary result of contemporary manifestations of internal contradictions in the world capitalist system.'   Thus in terms of political

organization, incorporation and segregation of some states and
organizations may be seen in relation to problems of integration
or development of others.

So far as an historical analysis of the protective roles of
states can be advanced the possibilities of the disintegration and
emergence of organizations will crucially relate to the character
of withdrawal or intrusion of protective administrative, military
or legal apparatuses. Some of these may be forced out by competing
agencies and others mobilized or demobilized because of pressures
arising from international economic considerations or political
alignments which convey their own protective capacities.

NOTES

We are indebted to Nicci Shannon for help in preparing this paper.
1 The consequence of this kind of definition is concern with any
   social or psychological mechanisms that may enhance or retard
   the achievement of such objectives. The determination of
   specification of objectives can be only a secondary question
   relying on the initial acceptance of what have presumably become
   dominant ones. A further implication, that productive mechanisms of organizational analysis have almost always been seen in
   terms of integration and co-operation in contrast to domination,
   is explored in relation to Human Relations, Scientific Management and Modern Organizational Theories by Allen (1975).
2 Perrow also assures us that in relating outputs to inputs
   (however defined) all organizations seek to minimize the impact
   of external organizational influences and to control as much as
   possible the uncertainties and variabilities of the environment.
   The thrust in organizations, he says, is towards routinization,
   standardization and bureaucracy - a trend that is inherent in
   the nature of an industrial civilization (Perrow, 1970,
   pp.178-9).
3 Thompson conceives organizations as open systems, hence indeterminate and faced with uncertainty, but at the same time as subject to criteria of rationality and therefore needing deter-
   minacy and certainty (p.10,13). As with Perrow, organizational
   rationality involves acquiring inputs and dispensing outputs in
   the smoothest or most competitive way.
4 The problem is especially pervasive when systems exchange concepts form part of the framework. In this case, as one writer
   summarizes it, all things seem to be possible:
       there are interdependencies not only between the part of the
       system, but also between the parts and objects of the envir-
       onment.... Accordingly, if elements in the enterprise's
       environment are changing, then, its actors may react by
       changing their behaviour.... This poses the problem of bound-
       ary determination, that is of delimiting which objects are
       to be considered as parts of the system and which as parts of
       the environment. There does not appear to be any clear
       solution to this problem when patterns of human interaction
       are involved, because actors who are members of any parti-
       cular system are themselves likely to be members of other

systems, and there will be interdependencies between their
behaviour in all systems (see Gilbert (ed.), 1972, p.30).

5   George Homans, for example, relies on such notions in his influential article Social Behaviour as Exchange (Homans, 1958).
Also Peter Blau proposes: 'Differentiation of power arises in
the course of competition for scarce goods.   In informal
groups, the initial competition is for participation time, which
is scarce, and which is needed to obtain any social reward from
group membership.   In communities the primitive competition is
for scarce means of livelihood' (see Blau, 1964, p.141).

The need to rely on this kind of explanation is rooted in
prevalent conceptions of exchange implying essentially that all
social relations entail ties by mutual dependence, and thereby
exclude consideration of power by definition.

Thus, in an influential book we find that,
The members of an organization contribute to the organization
in return for inducements that the organization offers them.
The contributions of one group are the source of the inducements that the organization offers them.   If the sum of the
contributions is sufficient, in quantity and kind, to supply
the necessary quantity and kinds of inducements, the organization survives and grows;   otherwise it shrinks and ultimately disappears unless an equilibrium is reached   (Simon,
1957, p.111).

6   For an analysis of this situation in terms of modern American
society see the essay by Barrington-Moore Jr, Some Prospects
for Predatory Democracy (Barrington-Moore, 1972, pp.150-93).

7   A classification in terms of bases of compliance and control
ranging from moral to coercive is devised by Etzioni (1961).
As a dynamic hypothesis Etzioni suggests that the kind of commitment and involvement forthcoming from members in the organization will vary depending on the nature of the power means -
coercive, remunerative or normative - that are mobilized.

For a classification of organizations in terms of who benefits from their activities see Blau and Scott (1963).   Blau
and Scott also emphasize that the various groups who make contributions to an organization do so in return for certain benefits received:
Thus the owners, the employees, and the customers of a business concern must each receive some recompense for their
various contributions; otherwise, they would not provide the
investment capital, the labour power, or the purchase price
for goods, all of which are necessary for the firm's continued operation.   The public at large also benefits from the
contribution that business concerns make to the 'general
welfare', specifically, to the production and distribution
of desired goods, and this benefit is the reason why the
society permits and encourages such firms to operate (1963,
pp.43-4).
For some reason, it might be added, Blau and Scott do not concern themselves with the contrary question: 'Who, in all this,
does not benefit?'

A number of schools concentrating variously on structural or
technological or environmental characteristics as major deter-

minants of organization (behaviour) has produced empirical investigations over the past ten years in 'Administrative Science Quarterly'.

8 See especially Wallerstein (1974) where it is argued that a world system encompassing empires, city states, and emerging 'nation-states' emerged in the sixteenth century based on a worldwide economic division of labour. Wallerstein characterizes the world system as

> one that has boundaries, structures, member groups, rules of legitimation and coherence. Its life is made up of the conflicting forces which hold it together by tension, and tear it apart as each group seeks eternally to remould it to its advantage. It has the characteristics of an organism, in that it has a life span over which its characteristics change in some respects and remain stable in others. One can define its structures as being at different times strong or weak in terms of the internal logic of its functioning (op. cit., p.347).

9 Also see the articles by Lane on The Economic Meaning of War and Protection and The Economic Consequences of Organized Violence (Lane, 1966). A suggestive discussion of the operation of protection as a means of expropriation of peasant surplus is given in an essay by Hilton in Landsberger (1974).

10 A good introductory discussion of the different ways feudalism has dissolved is given by Kay (1974, pp.69-98). For expropriation and consequent insurrection in England see, especially, Hilton (1973).

11 Under such conditions there were no doubt numerous queries about the efficacy of the state: the gardener's servant in King Richard II (Act III, Scene IV) asks:

> Why should we, in the compass of a pale,
> Keep law and form and due proportion,
> Showing as in a model, our firm estate,
> When our sea-walled garden, the whole land,
> Is full of weeds; her fairest flowers chok'd up,
> Her fruit trees all unprun'd, her hedges ruin'd,
> Her knots disorder'd, and her wholesome herbs
> Swarming with caterpillars?

12 The history of the impact of overseas colonialism on the formation and relation of European states is dealt with generally in Wallerstein (1974). Particularly good discussions are Boxer (1969), Parry (1963) and Elliot (1970).

13 For an account of the rise of one para-military organization and its rivalry with others see Boulton (1973). For a discussion of the position of the Irish Republican Army see Bell (1970), especially part VI.

14 As Fisk points out, it was only half-jokingly that strike leaders started naming their members as Minister of Agriculture, or Fuel, etc. P. Devlin, Minister of Health and Social Services in the Executive, described the strike as, 'an unadulterated coup d'etat for political reasons and was carried out in front of an inert combined security force of over 30,000' (see Devlin, 1975, p.15).

15 Sahlins provides a useful discussion of this point in his essay The Spirit of the Gift (Sahlins, 1974, pp.149-83).

Chapter 6

THE POWERLESSNESS
OF ORGANIZATION THEORY

Arthur Wassenberg

The key point is the discretion which market power provides in
choosing among alternative price, innovation, investment and other
strategies.   Firms which have no such latitude do not possess
market power.

(Shepherd, 1970, p.3)

Weak scale economies combined with relative stability and a high
ratio of inside-to-outside knowledge will strongly favour the development of collusion and other informal structure among independent
firms, rather than their consolidation into a dominant firm.   Evidently, the possible combinations are numerous and complex.

(Shepherd, 1970, p.39)

Outside the field of public utilities the position of a single
seller can in general be conquered - and retained for decades -
only on the condition that he does not behave like a monopolist.

(Schumpeter, 1970, p.99)

Die Innen-Auszen-Eifferenz ermöglicht es, Inseln geringerer komplex-
ität in der Welt zu bilden und zu erhalten.   (The inside-outside-
differentiation allows for the formation and maintenance of islands
of reduced complexity in the world.)

(Luhmann, 1970, p.116)

ISOLATIONISM OF ORGANIZATION THEORY

One of the more recent and alarming illustrations of the political
isolationism of organizations and administrative sciences to date
is their inability to comment in any systematic way on the economic
depression in industrialized capitalist states.   The economic state
of the nation influences the stability of the political system which
in its turn determines the structural setting in which individual
economic agents choose their priorities and strategies.   Neither
on the macro- nor on the micro-level of analysis of the contingencies between economic and political systems do the organization
sciences play an enlightening role.   Organization theory has gradu-

ally lost its analytical capacity and interest in the impact of
societal forces on the functioning of all kinds of formal organizations. As a consequence, the imporverished branch of general
sociology that is called organization theory finds itself unable
to explain the macro-consequences of the behaviour of that multitude
of organizations that comprises a society which is more or less con-
sciously bound in institutional frameworks. It is our contention
that only by reintroducing the institutional framework - that is by
infusing insights and ambitions from economic and political sociology - that organization theory may restore some of its intellectual and policy-oriented flavour.

The irony of recent history shows that the overly instrumental
orientation of organization theory gradually undermined its intellectual capacity. This neglect has led to a greater degree of
theoretical indifference in an empirical context that seems to be
increasingly marked by interdependence, complexity and the dialectics of politicization and professionalization. The blindness of
organization theory is one consequence of this.

The dominant theme in this paper is the proposition that organization behaviour can only be understood from a stratified and
dynamic perspective. The term 'stratified' refers to the multiple,
sometimes converging, hierarchies of interdependence in which organizations function. The term 'dynamic' refers to the possibly
impressive discrepancies between the de facto existence of structural interdependence between organizations and the cultural recognition and acceptance of those interdependencies. In particular,
the consequences of this incongruency·between structure and culture,
between factual dependence and culturally recognized or politically
legitimized dependence, lie at the heart of our comprehension of why
organizations differ in manoeuvrability, why organizations differ
in the capacity to afford not to learn, yet still manage to survive
successfully within their own criteria, and why some organizations
are more vulnerable to institutional weakness or failure than
others.

SOME EMPIRICAL OBSERVATIONS

Nation states continue to maintain and even multiply their *nation-
ally* oriented instruments and institutions which are designed for
the national control of their economies. This occurs in spite of
internationalization of markets for factors of production and for
goods and services, and despite a growth in the volume of world
trade which is two times faster than the volume of production of
most industrialized countries. This is surpassed by the subsid-
iaries of multi-national corporations and by an even faster growing
Euro-dollar market.

De Jong (1975), in a comparison of nineteenth-century reactions
to the preceding era of trade liberalization and growth of world
trade, which comprised the strategies of cartellization, protectionism and political isolationism, refers in this general context
to five more specific trends that will deeply influence the structure of European economies and consequently the structure, conduct
and performance of individual organizations, in particular private
enterprise.

First, the western countries show a slackening increase in their
population.   Despite uncertainties in demographic predictions, it
can be assumed that the 'biological recession' will last a longer
time than the economic one.   Second, there is a relative stagnation
in the output of industries producing durable consumption goods.
This may be attributed to increasing awareness of the deterioration
of the physical environment, rises in labour costs and the diminishing benefits of increasing the scale of production.   In particular, the construction and automotive industries in the USA and
the EEC suffer from market saturation and this, in turn, will have
a strong negative impact on other technologically and commercially
connected sectors.

Third, entrepreneurial strategies will show a more selective
innovation policy and adjustment to shifts in the ratios of pur-
chasing power.   Reorientation on the input-side (substitution of
production factors, lower prices, recycling, inventory control) as
well as on the output-side (reputation, marketing, product differentiation) will be more heavily emphasized.   Besides a more critically oriented consumer - a fourth trend - a final factor can be
mentioned.   Firms will concentrate more systematically on market
shares when the growth rate of the total economy or sectors therein
declines.   By technological, distributional and image-building
innovations, firms will embrace a stable or expanding market share
as an overwhelming objective in order to warrant a satisfactory
return on investment.

In short, a triple coincidence - decreased expansion, heightened
competition and cost rises - will characterize the immediate future.
This means an irrevocably extensive shift in interorganizational
relationships.   This will be seen horizontally between competitors,
and between factor suppliers, and vertically, between government
and private institutional partners.   A consequence of this will be
the increasing complexity and volatility of ad hoc coalition-
building *within* the three estates of capital, labour and government.

In such a context organization theory should develop its capacity
to describe and explain the relationships between internal organizational dynamics and the interorganizational games of coalition-
building, avoidance (i.e. protectionism and isolationism) and
obstruction.

For a theory of organization in a societal context, the basic
distributive-integrative principles and the substantive-institu-
tional elements (i.e. decision-making and decision-implementing
units) governing the authoritative allocation of values, will come
under heavy pressure.   Pressure emanates from the fact that the
stakes that the institutional partners (governments, labour, capital) control by mutual hostage, change deeply both in type and in
intensity.   Specifically, under these conditions, organization
theory should (after Ostrom, 1974, p.55):

1 anticipate the consequences which follow when
2 self-interested organizations choose maximizing strategies
   within
3 particular organizational arrangements and
4 particular structures of events

THEORY DEVELOPMENT

Three fairly recent schools of sociological reasoning can be seen
to play a constructive role in the type of organization-environment
problems we have briefly sketched.   First, the literature on interorganizational networks.   We may discern two schools of thought:
on the one hand the analogies and categorizations developed from
the earlier *intra*organizational theorizing on interdepartmental
relationships and aspects of decision-making;   on the other hand,
there is the extension of network theory and methodology to a poli-
tical-economy analysis of resource-sharing, domain and territory
conflict and accommodation/disruption strategies of organizations
vis-à-vis each other (Benson, 1975).
    Although there is still little empirical work available which
develops this theory and in which parts of theories have been
tested, the bulk of research is on the continuum of *competitive/
co-operative* relationships between more or less *similar* organizations involved in *horizontal* interaction porcesses (Aldrich, 1974,
1975; Marret, 1971).
    This type of exercise is reminiscent of the second orientation
we wish to mention here, namely the analysis of social power and
interaction processes conceived as *exchange* processes.   The emphasis here is not on the network as such, but on *individual* focal
organizations interacting with a more or less organized, segmented
or specialized environment.   Good examples of this tradition are
to be found in Dill (1958), Levine and White (1961) and Evan (1966).
This literature covers subjects such as the identification of relevant external factors with which an organization co-defines its
task environments, the varying degree of consensus in these co-
definitions (domain consensus) and the extension of Merton's ideas
about role-sets, sanctions and rewards to organizations as role
incumbents involved in exchanges of resources, prestige, and compliance.   With a few exceptions, however, the horizontal and equilibrium perspective predominates in these efforts, thus forgetting
Blau's notion that organizations are controlled by those who comprise or control the organization's most problematic dependencies
(Jacobs, 1974, p.53).
    Unfortunately, the basic notion of *emergence* of (power) struc-
tures from the processes of ongoing exchanges disappears completely
when it is transposed from the original intraorganizational focus
on socio-psychological processes to the interorganizational field
of socio-economic and socio-political phenomena.   Exchanges between
organizations become seen as the fruits of some Durkheimian division
of labour, resources, and expertise in a functional framework,
rather than as the consequences and cause of a *stratification* of
organizations in terms of power, prestige and resourcefulness
(Stinchcombe, 1965).
    A third approach is the somewhat ambiguously labelled contingency
theory, developed from the seminal ideas of Woodward, and Burns and
Stalker, and established under that name by Lawrence and Lorsch
(1967).   This approach aims to identify the structural correlates
between differentiation and integration and environmental characteristics such as complexity, heterogeneity, and turbulence in
economic and technological respects.

Replications of the findings of Lawrence, Lorsch and other scholars have cast serious doubts on the *intrinsic* validity and reliability of this contingency research.   In particular, Pennings
(1975), by reconsidering his own results has hinted at a reconstruction of the initial problematic.   This may be interpreted as a
prelude to more essential, *extrinsic* criticisms.   Interestingly,
these shortcomings echo the flaws of the first two 'schools' discussed previously.

The strong environmental correlates to organizational structure
as defended by contingency theorists may only hold for work organizations that have a stronger degree of (e.g. sequential or reciprocal) interdependence.   In short, the type of interdependence in
the internal work flow of organizations should be handled as an
important mediating variable in any comparative contingency analysis.   It would be appropriate, however, to ask for further refinements in which, on the one hand, organizational sensitivity to
environmental uncertainties is seen as the result of the interplay
of technological varieties of interdependence with varieties of
power structures within organizations.   On the other hand, environmental sensitivity is conceived as the result of strategies of
organizations directed at influencing the parameters of reciprocal,
sequential and pooled interdependence.   Organizations are simultaneously involved in the three types of interdependence.   However,
organizations can be contrasted in terms of the relative salience
of one of the three, and may be assumed to choose strategies to
gain an optimal mix of the three dependencies in order to improve
their net manoeuvrability.

CONCEPTUAL REORIENTATION

The criticism on the available approaches to organization-environment dynamics can be summarized as follows.   Interorganization,
exchange and contingency theories are biased in their attention to
horizontal, competitive, co-operative, countervailing and equili-
brium-seeking processes.   Moreover, these theories are overcom-
mitted to intraorganizational distinctions and refinements.   This
neglects the exploration and identification of the multi-dimension-
ality of the relevant environment of organizations.   Finally, the
wealth of insights provided by economics and political science
about concentration, oligopolistic competition, diversification,
innovation, technological and informational economies of scale,
coalition-building and political varieties of cartellization between
private and public power are left unused by the theories.   This
substantially weakens their comparative capacity in a double sense.

First, comparative organizational sociology is not derived from
a systematic evaluation of the impact of different environments,
structurally differing in time and in place.   Comparisons have
been based on differences in technology, and modes of differentiation and control in a task or technocratically oriented sense.
The latter are only linked by loosely defined concepts of the environment as a market and as a supplier of scientific novelties.
Even the notion of non-linear, step-function and time-lagged contingencies between environmental stimuli and organizational res-

ponses does not appear.   Second, comparative analysis does not
proceed by translating ideas about how organizations *differ* in their
environmental qualities into insights about how differently equipped
organizations interact with each other.   We may gain something of
the flavour of what economists and political scientists interested
in industrial organization have to offer in this realm from the
quotations at the beginning of this chapter.

The notion of time-lagged contingencies implies a general context
in which there is a high probability that there will be cultural and
structural lags.   Some of these will benefit, disadvantage or even
suppress some types of organizational behaviour and interests at the
expense of others.   Within this framework, we intend to pay special
attention to the transactional aspect of interorganizational reality.   We wish to raise some questions: How do organizations get
involved in transactions when differing in managerial and political
discretion?   How are managerial and political discretion contingent
upon lags and screens between structural interdependence and cultural awareness and moral acceptance of that interdependence?   This
type of conceptualization is aimed at introducing a *double* circu-
larity into the analysis.

First, the theory should be able to explain discretionary margins
of organizations in their mutual but not necessarily symmetric
transactions which emerge from structural-cultural lags.   Addition-
ally, it should try to explain how these margins in organizational
manoeuvrability are structurally made in contingencies that intend
to reinforce advantageous lags and to reduce disadvantageous ones.
Second, the theory should be able to derive propositions on the
*intra*organizational distributions of power, professional knowledge
and budgetary allocations *from* interorganizational dependencies
(structurally as well as culturally defined).   It should also be
able to predict the consequences from this multi-dimensional *intra*-
organizational set of characteristics for the environmental concern
and interorganizational strategies of individual organizations.

This approach resonates with Ostrom's plea in favour of a merger
between political and administrative science as seen above.   The
relevance of this transactional approach seems especially conspi-
cuous in the socio-economic and politico-administrative conditions
prevailing in western market or mixed economies after the oil
crisis.   These conditions are not listed to provide a ready-made
set of testable propositions on organizational behaviour.   They are
descriptive and provide symptomatic evidence for the myopia of the
sociology of organizations as it is exemplified by its latest
developments, namely the contingency approach to the covariance of
organizational and environmental characteristics.

At the same time, the field of social and political economic
dynamics may serve as a remedial example of the three main shortcomings of organizational sociology.   We would argue that these
are, first, a one-sided attention to comparative problems which
has resulted in the neglect of organizational interactions and
transactions; second, neglect of the 'stratification' problem; and
third, prevailing organization theories seem not to be alert to
the pitfalls of correlational and multivariate analysis of the relationships between organization and environment.   This last point
refers to the easily forgotten fact that adaptation, if any, of

organization structures to environmental conditions, takes time.
Also, organizational changes in structure and strategy influence
the state of the environment, provided we take appropriate time
lags into account and provided we accept the thesis that organizations do try to influence their environment instead of merely
responding to the latter in a satisficing or buffering mode.

This implies a three-step flow analysis of: environmental
stimuli-selective organizational responses in strategy and structure; and changes in the structure of the environment and in the
effect of environment stimuli, rather than a time-and-motionless
correlational contingency analysis.

From this threefold criticism of the state of affairs in organization theory emerges the broader institutional perspective, expres-
sing the pre-eminence of the structural and cultural lags in the
multi-organizational reality of industrialized society. Resource-
based interdependence between organizations and organized interest
groups may continue to increase without concomitant and equivalent
changes in the cultural state-of-readiness and the political reper-
toire of intelligence and control instruments to understand and
govern that interdependence. What matters is the absence of an
integrated theory based on the basic contention that organizations
and interests differ in their relative vulnerability to the lags
between structural interdependences and cultural repertoires for
recognizing and handling that interdependence.

It is our strong conviction that organization theory is deemed
to remain meaningless in the scientific as well as in the policy-
oriented sense when cut off from an institutional backing which
stresses the inequalities in the distribution of opportunities and
threats stemming from lags.   At most, it serves to consolidate
the unequal distribution of 'pluralistic' ignorance and hence the
unequal distribution of the organizational or institutional capacity
to afford not to learn.

The reason for linking this theoretical discussion of organization theory to a short overview of the most manifest characteristics of the economic crisis lies in its revealing character.
What a broad-scale crisis of this type reveals is the underlying
rules of the game that organizations play vis-à-vis each other. In
times of prosperity and expansion, problem-solving in the face of
'given' goals and of imbalances in the availability of countervailing power tends to fade away in an overall euphoria of the type
that Walton and McKersie (1965) named *integrative* bargaining. Only
'new scarcities' such as external effects to the physical environment play an important role in the public discussion of the balance
between the private and collective virtues of organizational goals
and strategies.

In times of stagnation, however, the 'old scarcities', especially
the meta-question of the distribution of decision-making power on
the allocation of societal values, appear to retain their classic
character and vehemence.   The overall climate tends towards *distributive* bargaining, including bargaining even on the rules of the
game.

Where organizations are subject to increasing, internationalized
interdependence, and where the political repertoires appropriate to
this development have been neglected, then crisis has a decisive

effect.   The lags and discrepancies, which occur will reveal the
essentially unchanged rules of the interorganizational games.
These games are formed by internal distributions of power, knowledge
and resources, induced by external interdependencies, the intervention of which may progressively change the parameters of the
task environment of organizations.

Times of depression and crisis enhance our understanding of
interventionist strategies.   They increase the visibility of
inequalities in the societal distribution of opportunities for
intervention and for pre-emptive action.   The theoretical effect of
this empirical reality should be to compensate for the passivity of
and stress on features such as 'buffering-zones' which have developed in recent decades.   Ironically, it is these decades that
produced an unparalleled upswing in mergers, technological economies
of scale, concentration ratios, emergence and decline of complete
industries and a growing acceleration of interaction between big
government and big enterprise.

It therefore seems justified to substitute Schumpeter's activist
notion of creative destruction for Simon's notions of satisficing
and Thompson's buffering-zones and negotiated orders as themes and
as principles of 'successful' organizations.   In summary, thus
far, for sociologists this overview stresses the urgency of rebuil-
ding the analysis in the direction of *transactional* and *stratifi-
cational* concepts.

This was previously labelled an *institutional* perspective in
which organizations are placed in an interorganizational context
which enables two classic sociological questions to be posed:

1 How do transactions between organizations influence the stratification of organizations in an institutional sector (e.g. the
  socio-economic and politico-economic subsystems of industrial
  society in times of industrial reconstruction)?

2 What structural (i.e. reciprocal, sequential, pooled interdependence) properties and what cultural (i.e. intellectual and political decision-making and evaluation) principles govern the evolution and devolution of that stratification of organizations?

More generally organization theory could then concentrate on the
analysis of two opposing forces that involve all organizations in
the socio- and politico-economic realm.   Briefly, the empirical
observables of the economic system to date are decreasing expansion,
increasing competition and the reappearance of old scarcities on a
higher level of large-scale production and distribution.   We may
expect, as a corollary, a stronger emphasis on the need of professionalization or technocratization as well as a stronger tendency
of politicization of all kinds of 'non-political' organizations, or
organized interest groups, and tripartite bargaining arenas in which
government, labour and capital meet.

Politicization may be circumscribed as an increase in endeavours
to shape society purposely by means of power-wielding (Hoogerwerf,
1975 p.178).   In terms of the foregoing analysis, power-wielding
is performed by (a) criticizing the political rules that govern
organizational stratification, and hence the terms of the balance
of transactions between organizations and organized interests within
the stratification, and/or by (b) endeavours to change the absolute
amount and relative distribution of the three types of structural

interdependence previously distinguished.   What seems to be essential is that politicization in its cultural as well as its structural manifestation tends to be boundary-emasculating in so far as
a clear cut demarcation of competences, eligibilities, domains, and
externalities between organizations is increasingly disputed and
actively attacked.

Whereas politicization emasculates existing boundaries between
organizations and strata, professionalization stresses the non-
political, expertise-based control of complexities and interdependencies in industrialized society.   In this situation an 'objective' division of labour and decision-making power should correspond
to the 'objective' problem-interdependencies that society has to
'solve'.   Conflicts in the latter perspective are essentially
interpreted as caused by lack of insights, lack of transparence of
the system-ness of society, and by incompatibilities between long-
term and short-term objectives and possibilities.   Solutions to
problems are unduly blocked by the inexorable inclination of interest groups to translate 'functional' problems of the division of
labour into political problems of the division of stakes, be they
commitments or rewards.

In this ideal-typical contrast between politicization (propensity
to emasculate boundaries) and professionalization (propensity to
identify and reify boundaries) a complete grouping of fashionable
phenomena characterizing organizational behaviour can be distinguished.   These phenomena comprise such dilemmas as internationalization of firms versus institution- (or constituency-) bound
nationalism and protectionism of government and unions;   centra-
lization of government in its endeavours to fight structural unemployment and regional depression, and to re-animate an ailing
economy, versus decentralization of diversifying firms and grass-
root pressure in labour unions to allow for more autonomy and flexibility of lower echelon tactics and strategies;   differentiation
of industry- or region-specific requirements seeking for more differentiated economic policies, versus integration of joint ventures
and collusive devices in mature oligopolies as strategies for
fighting uncertainties inherent in market saturation, slackening
economic growth, large-scale interdependencies at vertical integration.

What is important in this field of structural and strategic
contradictions is the mix of defensive and offensive strategies of
individual organizations.   The defensive activities can be described in their most general form as buffering and boundary-
screening by professionalization.   The offensive activities refer
to politicization which tends towards boundary emasculation.   The
basic axiom states that organizations will try to arrive at a
negotiated environment by decomposing that environment into pro-
fessionally 'problem-relevant' segments and by trying to force or
persuade the environment to accept this professional segmentation
of issues and stakes.

Simultaneously, however, organizations try to use the profession-
ally negotiated order as the grounds for the creative destruction of
existing boundaries by political claims.   Professional, legal-
rational standards of law and order in the division of assets and
liabilities tend to be denounced as politically biased and disad-

vantageous in themselves.   An example of this is where government
asks for the acceptance of principles of industrial or economic
democracy in the firm but meets managerial and entrepreneurial opposition which states that profit or limited-purpose organizations
are supposed to be governed by instrumental criteria of efficiency
rather than by the ideological aegis of the collective good.   High-
lighting the differences between requirements of democracy and those
of goal-specific efficiency, however, does not prevent private
management from repeating the exhortation that government and public
bureaucracy should embrace the basics of professional management
and that they should learn from private experience, expertise and
business acumen instead of continuing to be at the mercy of the
excess demands of a collection of interest groups.   Each emphasizes
the 'matter-of-fact' limits of its own responsibilities and commitments.

A realistic organization theory should spell out the structural
correlates and the strategic subtleties in organizational conduct
given two conditions: first, organizations are asymmetrically
interdependent in that they differ in their bases of power, the
amount or weight of power, and the reach or breadth of power;
second, organizations use their powers on different levels of interest aggregation in that they strive for interest representation
and defence on that level where the mix of reciprocal, sequential
and pooled interdependence approaches a theoretical optimum of
manoeuvrability.

Manoeuvrability is an organizational specimen of the general
Weberian concept of power: the chance of acquiring and maintaining
the capacity to influence the parameters of the behaviour of others
in accordance with the objectives of the actor.   The main problem
for the theorist, however, in analysing the complexities of the
welfare state, is the puzzling *indirectness* of the process of
influence-wielding and effective sanctioning.

Manoeuvrability is the outcome of the structural position in the
web of reciprocal, sequential and pooled interdependencies.   In
this vein, Luhmann's version of the reduction of complexity - the
emergence of enclaves of reduced complexity by designing and enforcing inside-outside boundaries - regains *political* flavour.

Do organizations differ in their capacity to reduce (for themselves, rather than for the 'world') complexity and, at the same
time, succeed in maintaining complexity for their institutional
counterparts? If the answer is yes, and if we are able to elaborate
the power implications of the differential distribution of capacities to reduce complexity in the societal stratification of organizations, we learn something about the manoeuvrability of organizations.   When we know more about this we have, both intellectually
and politically, a better base for speculation about the contingencies between environmental conditions and the intraorganizational
twin of strategy and structure.

Compared to sociologists, economists are far ahead in spelling
out the modalities of pooled, sequential and reciprocal interdependence in situations of less-than-perfect competition (Scherer,
1970; Shepherd, 1970; Jaquemin and de Jong, 1976).   In consequence,
sociologists and political scientists should rephrase their insights
into the sociological correlates of bounded rationality, environ-

mental complexity and illiberality (Child, 1972).   They must also
consider the political correlates of voluntarism in the mixed
market economy for the feasibility of 'polycentric' (Gregg, 1974)
decision-making by public authorities, in order to reach a better
correspondence with the economists of industrial organization
dynamics.

DISCUSSION: CENTRAL CONCEPTS AND RESEARCH

A recent study by Staw and Szwajkowski (1975) is suggestive of a
fruitful co-operation between the three disciplines in the analysis
of the interplay of horizontal (intercursive) and vertical (inte-
gral) relationships between organizations.   The authors test the
hypothesis that the less munificent the organization's environment,
the more effort the organization will exert to obtain resources
from that environment, and the more likely it is that it will engage
in legally questionable activities.   Environmental scarcity (which
in this study was indicated by low financial performance, poor
demand for a given class of products, shortages of raw materials,
or widespread strikes) does appear to be related to a range of
officially registered trade violations such as price-fixing, illegal
mergers and acquisitions, refusal to deal, tying arrangements, fore-
closure of entry, etc.
    What is important is the systematization of findings about how
organizations choose modes of resource procurement and try to
enhance their manoeuvrability rather than engage in sealing off
their technological core.   Both topics are of substantial importance but the offensive categories of organizational behaviour
(choosing a strategy, choosing a structure) deserve special attention.   This will redress the balance of a period of more or less
exclusive engagement in the study of defensive examples of organizational behaviour.
    The systematization of scattered designs and findings may con-
ceptually follow three mutually supporting dimensions.   First,
economic and sociological literature on external organization relationships can be rephrased in terms of reciprocal, sequential and
pooled interdependence.   Characterizing organizations in terms of
their most critical dependencies, and in terms of the relevant mix
of the three types of interdependence may lead to a comparative list
of power bases (type of interdependence), of the weight or amount
of power, referring to the potential intensity and *indirectness* of
power-wielding, and of the range or reach of power (expressed by
the ideal-typical mixes of interdependence).   From this comparative
framework on the structure of interorganizational relationships we
can proceed to the transactional analysis of interorganizational
games.   This will involve starting with the varieties of transactions between organizations that we expect from comparable or
dissimilar mixes of interdependence.
    What this first conceptual dimension provides is the design of
a set of principles of bounded interdependence as they are supposed
to govern interorganizational relationships.   Of particular interest will be the possibilities for organizations to *change* the mix
of interdependence they are confronted with, in accordance with

their own objectives.   In a theory of self-interested organization
behaviour, changes in the mix of interdependence (horizontally as
well as vertically), in accordance with the organization's objectives are intended to enhance the organization's manoeuvrability
vis-à-vis other organizations.   Changes in manoeuvrability mean,
by definition, changes in power.   Thus, power is the (probability
of the) capacity to change the parameters (i.e. mix of interdependence) underlying *alter's* behaviour.

In addition we require an explication of *bounded rationality* and
bounded legitimacy.   The main contributions here come from political science and sociology: they refer, broadly speaking, to the
cultural dimension of power-games which underlie interorganizational
transactions.

Initially, we argued that the essential problem for the theory
of organizations was to (i) anticipate the consequences which follow
when (ii) self-interested organizations choose maximizing strategies
within (iii) particular organizational arrangements and (iv) particular structures of events.

We may now say that, thus far, only a first approximation of the
second and third elements has been offered, whereas the fourth point
has been touched upon only in a suggestive sense.   The first point
has been left completely unspecified.   In the context of this
chapter we have chosen as an exemplary 'structure of events' the
threefold problem of 'stagflation'.   This is characterized by high
price and cost increases, accompanied by the reappearance of old
scarcities and rigidities under conditions of large-scale production and distribution;   decreasing expansion rates and expansion
opportunities;   and increases in international 'market share' competition in numerous industries.   These encourage the retaliatory
risks of protectionism and create the possibility of serious tensions between labour, capital and government.   Each of them is
interested only in enhancing or maintaining its own manoeuvrability,
and hence is sensitive to circumvention of the brittle rules of
accommodation.

The third element in the above-mentioned paraphrase of the organization theory problem, 'particular organizational arrangements',
was dealt with by introducing the principle of bounded interdependence.   The structural base of manoeuvrability may be analysed by
the multi-level mix of three ideal-types of interdependence.
Besides this structural dimension, we need a double cultural dimension to be able to specify the institutional constraints within
which 'self-interested organizations choose maximizing strategies'.

The cultural constraints are the *bounds of rationality* - referring to the limited data-acquiring, data-processing and problem-
solving capacities of organizations in controlling their internal
and external environments - and the *bounds of legitimacy*, which
refers to a possibly broad margin between accountability per se and
pragmatic law-and-order enforcement in an industrial complex which
is becoming more opaque and interdependent and internationally dis-
ruptable.

The bounds of legitimacy refer to the culturally lagging capacity
to understand, monitor and take into account increasing structural
interdependencies.   The bounds of legitimacy may be seen at work
in a variety of settings from the separation of elites, audiences

and constituencies *within* interest groups to the separation *between*
inter-elite cartels (industry-government) and less well organized
collectivities (consumers, unemployed and dwellers of depressed
areas and urban slums).

The notion of the opposing forces called politicization versus
professionalization, constituted by the three principles of bounded
interdependence, rationality and legitimacy should help to clarify
how transactions between organizations occur.   This three-dimen-
sional model summarized in the dialectics of politicization and professionalization, offers a chance to restore the micro-macro framework to organizational sociology.

The *intra*organizational perspective has been left largely
untouched in this chapter.   This has been because the interorganizational perspective deserves disproportional energy in order to
construct a truly institutional contingency theory about the association between organizational structure and environmental conditions.   The linking concept is the organizational strategy.   Organizational strategy needs to be conceived and interpreted in a more
pro-active spirit than has been the case so far in organization
theory.   The emphasis lies on the structural and cultural constraints pertaining to self-interested organizations choosing strategies that maximize their manoeuvrability.

The concepts of politicization and professionalization may be
investigated in a number of ways.   One possibility would be an
industry-specific, comparative analysis of the dialectics of professionalization and politicization in the tripartite and multi-
level strategies of government, labour and capital.   Special
attention would have to be paid to the development of boundary-
spanning roles in each of the relevant institutional partners that
are tied together in mutually different mixes of interdependence.

The sociology of interorganizational structure, conduct and performance should be able to contribute some meaningful insights into
sequential dilemmas in a period of far-reaching industrial reconstruction.   The first step is the restoration of the concepts of
power and transaction in the theory of organizations.   The second
step is the operationalization of the principles of bounded interdependence, legitimacy and rationality.   The third step is the
spelling out of the following: the anticipation of the consequences
which follow when self-interested organizations choose strategies
to maximize manoeuvrability in interdependent arrangements in a
changing economic and political environment.

BIBLIOGRAPHY

ABELL, P. (1975), The Role of 'power' in Organization Theory: Discussion Issues, discussion paper presented to the session on Power and Organizations, European Group for Organization Studies (EGOS) Colloquium on Current Issues in Organizational Studies, Breau-sans-Nappe, France, 3-5 April 1975.

ALDRICH, H. (1974), An Interorganizational Dependency Perspective on Relations Between the Employment Service and its Organization Set, Mimeo NYSSILR, Cornell University.

ALDRICH, H. (1975), Relations Between Local Employment Service Offices and Social Service Sector Organizations, Mimeo NYSSILR, Cornell University.

ALLEN, V.L. (1975), 'Social Analysis: A Marxist Critique and Alternative', London, Longman.

ALTHUSSER, L. (1969), 'For Marx', translated by Ben Brewster, London, Allen Lane, The Penguin Press.

BACHRACH, P. and BARATZ, M.S. (1969), Two Faces of Power, 'American Political Science Review', vol.56, pp.947-52.

BACHRACH, P. and BARATZ, M.S. (1971), 'Power and Poverty', Oxford University Press.

BAIN, J.F. (1967), Chamberlain's Impact on Micro-Economic Theory', in R.E. Hughen (ed.), 'Monopolistic Competition Theory Studies in Impact', New York, Wiley, pp.147-76.

BARAN, P. (1973), 'The Political Economy of Growth', Harmondsworth, Penguin.

BARNARD, C.I. (1966), 'The Functions of the Executive', Cambridge, Mass., Harvard University Press.

BARRINGTON-MOORE Jr, G. (1972), 'Reflections on the Causes of Human Misery and Upon Certain Proposals to Eliminate Them', London, Allen Lane, The Penguin Press.

BAUMOL, N. (1959), 'Business Behaviour, Value and Growth', London, Macmillan.

BELL, B. (1970), 'The Secret Army', London, Blond.

BELL, C., FIRTH, R. and HARRIS, C. (1974), Review Symposium on 'The Symmetrical Family' (Young and Willmott), 'Sociology', vol.8, no.3.

BENNIS, W.G., BERKOWITZ, N., AFFINITO, M. and MALONE, M. (1958), Authority, Power and the Ability to Influence, 'Human Relations', vol.XI, no.2, pp.143-56.

99

BENSON, J.K. (1975), The Interorganizational Network as a Political Economy, ASQ, vol.20, pp.229-49.

BENYON, H. (1973), 'Working for Fords', Harmondsworth, Penguin.

BERGER, J. (1975), 'A Seventh Man', Harmondsworth, Penguin.

BERNAL, J.D. (1957), 'Science in History', Harmondsworth, Penguin.

BLACKMAN, J. (1969), The Campaign for Women's Rights, 1968, 'Trade Union Register', ed. Coates, Topham, Barratt Brown, London, Merlin.

BLAU, P. (1964), 'Exchange and Power in Scoial Life', New York, Wiley.

BLAU, P. (1968), Organizations, in 'The International Encyclopaedia of the Social Sciences', London, Macmillan and New York, Free Press.

BLAU, P. and SCOTT, W.R. (1963), 'Formal Organizations: A Comparative Approach', London, Routledge & Kegan Paul.

BLUM, A.F. (1974), Positive Thinking, 'Theory and Society', vol.I, part 3, pp.245-69.

BOSE, A. (1975), Marxian and Post-Marxian Political Economy, Harmondsworth, Penguin.

BOULTON, D. (1973), The U.V.F. 1966-73, Belfast, Torc Books.

BOURDIEU, P. (1975), The Specificity of the Scientific Field and the Social Conditions of the Progress of Reason, 'Social Science Information', vol.14, no.6. (page references in this text refer to pre-publication proof copy).

BOXER, C.R. (1969), 'The Portugese Seaborne Empire 1415-1825', London, Hutchinson.

BUTLER, R.J., HICKSON, D.J. and McCULLOUGH, A.E. (1974), Power in the Organizational Coalition, paper presented to the World Congress of Sociology, Research in Organizations Section, at Toronto, Canada, August 1974.

CENTRAL OFFICE OF INFORMATION (1975), Women in Britain, Reference Pamphlet 67, London, HMSO.

CHAMBERLIN, E. (1953), 'A Theorie de la concurrence monopolistique', Paris, PUF.

CHILD, J. (1972), Organization Structure, Environment and Performance: the Role of Strategic Choice, 'Sociology', 6, pp.1-22.

CLEGG, S. (1975), 'Power, Rule and Domination: A Critical and Empirical Understanding of Power in Sociological Theory and Organizational Life', London, Routledge & Kegan Paul.

CLEGG, S. (1976), Power, Theorizing and Nihilism, 'Theory and Society', vol.I, part 3, pp.65-87.

COLE, G.D.H. (1957), Introduction to 'Capital' by Karl Marx, vol.1, translated from the Fourth German Edition by Eden and Cedar Paul, London, Dent, Everyman Library.

COMER, L. (1974), 'Wedlocked Women', Leeds, Feminist Books.

Conservative Government Consultative Document (1973), 'Equal Opportunities for Men and Women', London, HMSO.

CROCKER, L. (1973), Marx's Concept of Exploitation, 'Social Theory and Practice', pp.201-15.

CROZIER, M. (1964), 'The Bureaucratic Phenomena', London, Tavistock.

CYERT, R.M. and MARCH, J.G. (1963), 'A Behavioural Theory of the Firm', Englewood Cliffs, New Jersey, Prentice-Hall.

DAHL, R.A. (1957), The Concept of Power, 'Behavioural Science', vol.2, pp.201-15.

DAUMAS, M. (1957), 'Histoire de la science', Paris, Gallimard.

DAUMAS, M. (1962, 1965, 1968), 'Histoire générale des techniques', 3 vols, Paris, PUF.

DEPARTMENT OF EMPLOYMENT (1974a), 'Women and Work.   A Statistical Survey', Manpower Paper No. 9, London, HMSO.
DEPARTMENT OF EMPLOYMENT (1974b), 'Women and Work.   Sex Differences and Society', Manpower Paper No. 10, London, HMSO.
DEPARTMENT OF EMPLOYMENT (1975), 'Women and Work.   A Review', Manpower Paper No. 11, London, HMSO.
DEVLIN, P. (1975), 'The Fall of the Executive', Harmondsworth, Penguin.
DILL, W.R. (1958), Environment as an Influence on Managerial Autonomy, 'ASQ', vol.2, pp.172-91.
DILLON, M. and LEHAHE, D. (1973), 'Political Murder in Northern Ireland', Harmondsworth, Penguin.
DUBIN, R. (1957), Power and Union - Management Relations, 'ASQ', vol.2, pp.60-81.
DUNKERLEY, D. (1972), 'The Study of Organizations', London, Routledge & Kegan Paul.
DUTT, R. (1903), 'The Economic History of India in the Victorian Age', vol.I, London, Routledge & Kegan Paul.
EASTON, D. (1967), 'A Systems Analysis of Political Life', London, Wiley.
EDWARDS, C.D. (1970), Conglomerate Bigness as a Source of Power, in Shepherd (1970).
ELLIOT, J.H. (1970), 'The Old World and the New 1492-1650', Cambridge University Press.
EMERY, F.E. and TRIST, E.L. (1965), The Causal Texture of Organizational Environments, 'Human Relations', vol.18, pp.21-32.
ENNIS, K. (no date), 'Women Fight Back', London, Woman's Voice Pamphlet.
Equal Pay Act (1970), London, HMSO.
ETZIONI, A. (1961), 'A Comparative Analysis of Complex Organizations', New York, Free Press.
EVAN, W.M. (1966), The Organization Set: Toward a Theory of Interorganizational Relations, in J.D. Thompson (ed.) 'Approaches to Organizational Design', University of Pittsburgh Press, pp.173-88.
FEUR, L.S. (ed.) (1969), 'Marx and Engels: Basic Writings on Politics and Philosophy', London, Collins, The Fontana Press.
FISK, R. (1975), 'The Point of No Return: The Strike Which Broke British Rule in Ulster', Times Books, London, André Deutsch.
FOGARTY, M., ALLEN, A.J., ALLEN, I. and WALTERS, P. (1971), 'Women in Top Jobs', Political and Economic Planning, London, Allen & Unwin.
FOGARTY, M., RAPOPORT, R. and RAPOPORT, R. (1971), 'Sex, Career and Family', Political and Economic Planning, London, Allen & Unwin.
FRANK, A.G. (1967), 'Capitalism and Underdevelopment in Latin America', New York, Monthly Review Press.
FRENCH, J.R.P. and RAVEN, B. (1959), The Bases of Social Power, in D. CARTWRIGHT (ed.), 'Studies in Social Power', Ann Arbor, University of Michigan.
FRIEDAN, B. (1965), 'The Feminine Mystique', London, Penguin.
GEIGER, T. (1964), 'Vorstudien zu einer Soziologie des Rechts', Berlin, Neuwied.
GILBERT, M. (ed.) (1972), 'The Modern Business Enterprise', Harmondsworth, Penguin.
GOULDNER, A. (1970), 'The Coming Crisis of Western Sociology', London, Heinemann.

GRAMSCI, A. (1971), 'Selections from the Prison Notebooks', edited
and translated by Quintin Hoare and Geoffrey Nowell Smith, London,
Lawrence & Wishart.

GRAMSCI, A. (1975), 'Letters from Prison', selected, translated and
introduced by Lynne Lawler, London, Cape.

GREGG, P.M. (1974), Units and Levels of Analysis: A Problem of
Policy Analysis in Federal Systems, 'Publius: the Journal of Feder-
alism', 4, pp.56-71.

HAGE, J. (1974), The State of Organizational Theory, American
Sociological Association, Section on Organizations paper.

HEISENBERG, W. (1962), 'La Nature dans la physique contemporaine',
Paris, Gallimard.

HICKSON, D.J., HININGS, C.R., LEE, C.A., SCHNECK, R.E. and
PENNINGS, J.M. (1971), A Strategic Contingencies Theory of Intra-
Organizational Power, 'ASQ', vol.16, no.2, pp.216-29.

HILL, C. (1969), 'The Century of Revolution: 1603-1713', London,
Sphere Books.

HILTON, R. (1973), 'Bond Men Made Free: Medieval Serfs in Medieval
England', London, Macmillan.

HININGS, C.R., HICKSON, D.J., PENNINGS, J.M. and SCHNECK, R.E.
(1974), Structural Conditions of Intra-Organizational Power, 'ASQ',
vol.19, no.1.

HIRSCH, P.M. (1975), Organizational Effectiveness and the Institutional Environment, 'ASQ', vol.20, pp.327-44.

HOBSBAWM, E.J. (1969), 'Industry and Empire', Harmondsworth,
Penguin.

HOMANS, G.C. (1958), Social Behaviour as Exchange, 'American Journal
of Sociology', vol.63, pp.597-606.

HOOGERWERF, A. (1975), Politisering, dogmatisme en confirmisme,
'Beleid en Maatschappij', 7/8.

HUNT, A. (1975), 'Management Attitudes and Practices Towards Women
at Work', London, HMSO.

JACOBS, D. (1974), Dependency and Vulnerability: An Exchange
Approach to the Control of Organizations, 'ASQ', vol.19, pp.45-59.

JAQUEMIN, A.P. and de JONG, H.W. (1976), 'Markets, Corporate
Behaviour and the State', Leiden, Stenfert Kroese.

JEPHCOTT, P., SEEAR, N. and SMITH, J.H. (1962) 'Married Women
Working', London, Allen & Unwin.

DE JONG, H.W. (1975), Het Economisch Klimaat, "Bedrijfskunde', 3

DE JONG, H.W. (forthcoming), 'Power, Profits and Wastage - our
Economic Analysis of the European Pharmaceutical Industry'.

DE JONG, H.W. and DE LANGE, R. (1975), Concentration in the Pharmaceutical Industry in the Netherlands, Mimeo, no place.

KARPIK, L. (1972), 'Les Politiques et les logiques d'action de la
grande entreprise industrielle', Sociologie du Travail, no.I,
pp.82-105.

KAY, C. (1974), 'Comparative Development of the European Manorial
System and the Latin American Hacienda System', 'Journal of Peasant
Studies', vol.2, no.I, pp.69-98.

KLEIN, V. (1965), 'Britain's Married Women Workers', London,
Routledge & Kegan Paul.

KUHN, T.S. (1962), The Structure of Scientific Revolutions, 'International Encyclopaedia of Unified Science', vol.2, no.2, London,
University of Chicago Press.

Labour Party Folder (1975), 'Women in Society - An Analysis',
London, The Labour Party.
Labour Party Green Paper (1972), 'Discrimination Against Women',
London, The Labour Party.
LANDSBERGER, H. (ed.) (1974), 'Rural Protest: Peasant Movements and
Social Change', London, Macmillan.
LANDSBERGER, H.A. (1958), 'Hawthorne Revisited', New York, Cornell
University Press.
LANE, F.C. (1966), 'Venice and History', Baltimore, Johns Hopkins
Press.
LAWRENCE, P.R. and LORSCH, J.W. (1967), 'Organization and Environ-
ment', Division of Research, Graduate School of Business Admini-
stration, Cambridge, Mass., Harvard University.
LENOBLE, R. (1957), Origines de la pensée scientifique moderne, in
DAUMAS (1957).
LEVINE, S. and WHITE, P.E.,(1961), Exchange as a Conceptual Frame-
work for the Study of Interorganizational Relationships, 'ASQ',
vol.5, pp.97-108.
LINDBLOM, C.E. (1959), The Science of Muddling Through, 'Public
Administration Review', vol.1, pp.13-31.
LIPSEY, R.G. (1963), 'An Introduction to Positive Economics',
London, Weidenfeld and Nicolson.
LLOYD, L. (1972), Women Workers in Britain: A Handbook, London,
Socialist Women Publications.
LUHMANN, N. (1970), 'Soziologische Aufklarung, Aufsatze zur Theorie
sozialer Systeme', Köln, Opladen.
LUKES, S. (1974), 'Power: A Radical View', London, Macmillan
Papermac.
MACPHERSON, C.B. (1962), 'The Political Theory of Possessive Indivi-
dualism', Oxford, Clarendon Press.
MACPHERSON, C.B. (1973), 'Democratic Theory: Essays in Retrieval',
Oxford, Clarendon Press.
MANSFIELD, C.B. (1968), 'The Economics of Technological Change',
New York, Norton.
MARCH, J.G. and SIMON, H.A. (1958), 'Organizations', New York,
Wiley.
MARCHINGTON, M.P. (1975a), A Path Model of Power Generation, The
University of Aston Management Centre Working Paper Series, no.36.
MARCHINGTON, M.P. (1975b), Sources of Work Group Power Capacity,
The University of Aston Management Centre Working Paper Series,
no.41.
MARCUSE, H. (1964), 'One-Dimensional Man: Studies in the Ideology of
Advanced Industrial Societies', London, Routledge & Kegan Paul.
MARRETT, C.B. (1971), On the Specification of Interorganizational
Dimensions, 'Sociology and Social Research', vol.56, pp.147-63.
MARRIS, R.A. (1961), 'Managerial Capitalism', New York, Free Press.
MARX, K. (1954), 'Capital', vol.1, Moscow, Foreign Languages
Publishing House.
MARX, K. (1957), 'Capital', vol.1, London, Dent, Everyman Library.
MARX, K. (1962), 'Capital', vol.3, Moscow, Foreign Languages
Publishing House.
MARX, K. (1965), 'Introduction générale à la critique de l'économie
politique', Paris, Gallimard.
MARX, K. (1969), 'The Eighteenth Brumaire of Louis Bonaparte', in
L.S. Feur (ed.) (1969).

104 Bibliography

MARX, K. (1973), 'Grundrisse: An Introduction to the Critique of
Political Economy', Harmondsworth, Penguin.
MASSE, P. (1965), 'Le Plan ou l'anti-hasard', Paris, Gallimard.
MEAD, M. (1935), 'Sex and Temperament in Three Primitive Societies',
London, Routledge & Kegan Paul.
MEAD, M. (1962), 'Male and Female', London, Allen Lane, The Penguin
Press.
MECHANIC, D. (1962), Sources of Power of Lower Participants in
Complex Organizations, 'ASQ', vol.7, pp.349-64.
MYRDAL, A. and KLEIN, V. (1956), 'Women's Two Roles: Home and Work',
London, Routledge & Kegan Paul.
NATIONAL COUNCIL FOR CIVIL LIBERTIES (1974a), 'Danger! Women at
Work', report on conference held on 16 February 1974, London.
NATIONAL COUNCIL FOR CIVIL LIBERTIES (1974b), 'Equality for Women',
comments on Labour government's proposals for anti-discrimination
legislation, London, NCCL.
NATIONAL COUNCIL FOR CIVIL LIBERTIES (1975), 'Equal Pay and How To
Get It', London, NCCL.
OAKLEY, A. (1972), 'Sex, Gender and Society', London, Temple Smith.
OAKLEY, A. (1974), 'Housewife', London, Allen Lane.
O'CONNOR, J. (1974), 'The Corporation and the State: Essays in the
Theory of Capitalism and Imperialism', New York, Harper Colophon
Books.
OSTROM, V. (1974), 'The Intellectual Crisis in American Public
Administration', Alabama University Press.
PAHL, R.E. and WINKLER, J.T. (1974), The Economic Elite: Theory
and Practice, in P. Stanworth and A. Gibbens (ed.), 'Elites and
Power in British Society', Cambridge University Press.
PARRY, G. and MORRISS, P. (1974), When is a Decision Not a Decision
Decision?, in I. CREWE (ed.), 'British Political Sociology Yearbook:
Elites in Western Democracy', vol.1, London, Crook Helm.
PARRY, J.H. (1963), 'The Age of Reconaissance: Discovery, Explora-
tion and Settlement 1450-1650', London, Weidenfeld & Nicolson.
PENNINGS, J.M. (1975), The Relevance of the Structural-Contingency
Model for Organizational Effectiveness, 'ASQ', vol.20, pp.393-410.
PERROUX, F. (1953), Introduction, in E. Chamberlin (1953), 'La
Théorie de la concurrence monopolistique', Paris, PUF.
PERROW, C. (1970), 'Organizational Analysis: A Sociological View',
London, Tavistock.
POLANYI, K. (1957), 'The Great Transformation', New York, Beacon
Press.
Report of the 44th TUC Woman Workers Conference (1974) (pp.30-8,
Comments of TUC General Council on Conservative Government's
Consultative Document 'Equal Opportunities for Men and Women')
RICHTA, R. (1969), 'La Civilization au carrefour', Paris, Anthropos.
ROETHLISBERGER, F.J. and DICKSON, W.J. (1939), 'Management and the
Worker', Cambridge, Mass., Harvard University Press.
ROGERS, J.T. (1920), 'The Industrial and Commercial History of
England', London, Fisher Unwin.
ROWTHORN, B. (1974), Neo-Ricardianism or Marxism?, 'New Left
Review', no.86, pp.63-87.
RUTTER, M. (1972), 'Maternal Deprivation Reassessed', Harmondsworth,
Penguin.
SAHLINS, M. (1974), 'Stone Age Economics', London, Tavistock.

SCHATTSCHNEIDER, E.E. (1960), 'The Semi-Sovereign People: A Realists View of Democracy in America', New York, Holt, Rinehart Winston.
SCHERER, F.M. (1970), 'Industrial Market Structure and Economic Performance', Chicago, Rand McNally.
SCHMOOKLER, J. (1966), 'Innovation and Economic Growth', Cambridge, Mass., Harvard University Press.
SCHUMPETER, J. (1970), 'Capitalism, Socialism and Democracy', London, Unwin University Books, London, Allen & Unwin.
SENSAT Jr, J. and CONSTANTINE, G. (1975), A Critique of the Foundations of Utility Theory, 'Science and Society', Summer, vol. XXXIX, no.2, pp.157-79.
Sex Discrimination Bill (1975), London, HMSO, March.
SHEPHERD, W.G. (1970), 'Market Power and Economic Welfare', New York, Random House.
SILVERMAN, D. (1970), 'The Theory of Organisations', London, Heinemann.
SILVERMAN, D. (1974), Speaking Seriously, 'Theory and Society',vol.I, nos 1,3.
SIMMEL, G. (1971), 'On Individuality and Social Forms', edited and with an introduction by K.H. Woolf, London, Free Press & Collier-Macmillan.
SIMON, H.A. (1957), 'Administrative Behaviour', New York, Macmillan.
SMITH, D.E. (1974), Women's Perspective as a Radical Critique of Sociology, 'Sociological Inquiry', vol.44, no.1.
SPANN, O. (1930), 'Types of Economic Theory', London, Allen & Unwin.
STAW, B.M. and SZAJKOWSKI, E. (1975), The Scarcity Munificence Component of Organizational Environments and the Commission of Illegal Acts, 'ASQ', vol.20, pp.345-54.
STINCHCOMBE, A.L. (1965), Social Structure and Organizations, in J.G. March (ed.), 'Handbook of Organizations', Chicago, Rand McNally, pp.142-93.
TANNENBAUM, A.S. (1968), 'Control in Organizations', New York, McGraw-Hill.
THOMPSON, J.D. (1956), Authority and Power in 'Identical' Organizations, 'AJS', LXII, pp.290-301.
THOMPSON, J.D. (1967), 'Organizations in Action', New York, McGraw-Hill.
TORODE, B. (1975), Interrupting Intersubjectivity, paper presented to the conference on 'The Experience of Schooling', Faculty of Educational Studies, Open University, April 1975.
TUC (1975), 'General Council's Report to Congress', Congress House, London.
WALLERSTEIN, I. (1974), 'The Modern World-System: Capitalist Agriculture and the Origins of the European World Economy in the Sixteenth Century', London, Academic Press.
WALTON, R.E. and MCKERSIE, R.B. (1965), 'Theory of Labour Negotiations; An Analysis of a Social Interaction System', New York, McGraw-Hill.
WEBER, M. (1947), 'The Theory of Social and Economic Organization', translated by T. Parsons and A.M. Henderson, with an introduction by T. Parsons, Chicago, Free Press.
WEBER, M. (1968), 'Economy and Society: An Outline of Interpretive Sociology', edited and with an introduction by G. Roth and C. Wittich, New York, Bedminster Press.

WEICK, K.E. (1969), 'The Social Psychology of Organizing', Reading, Mass., Addison-Wesley.

White Paper (1974),'Equality for Women', London, HMSO.

WILLIAMSON, O. (1963), A Model of Rational Managerial Behaviour, in CYERT, R.M. and MARCH, J.G. (1963).

WITTGENSTEIN, L. (1968), 'Philosophical Investigations', translated by G.E.M. Anscombe, Oxford, Blackwell.

YOUNG, M. and WILLMOTT, P. (1973),'The Symmetrical Family', London, Routledge & Kegan Paul.

INDEX